Endorsemen

Raw emotion, family pain, and ultimately sweet healing with hope of tomorrow. *Beyond the Scars'* raw honesty holds the reader in suspense until the final chapter. Unforgettable . . . a page turner.

—Donalyn Powell, author

In July of 2013, I interviewed Amy Collier on my radio show, *Wealthy Thoughts.* The world listened to the story of this brave and courageous woman. If you have also lived through abuse, pain, depression, and perhaps even attempts to end it all through suicide, you now have the answer. I strongly encourage you pick up a copy of Amy's book, *Beyond the Scars.* Amy holds your hand and shows you that love, happiness, success, and healthy relationships are yours when you take this first step toward freedom.

—Richard J. Levy,
author of *Thoughts Make You Wealthy,*
http://happinessmakessuccess.com

A compelling memoir of a true survivor who endured unspeakable mental, physical, and sexual abuse. Amy was stronger than her demons and clung to her faith through Matthew 19:16–26. This is her resonating account of how people are put in your life at the right time proving there are angels among us. A tender portrayal of strong faith, prayer, resilience, and proof that people can transcend beyond their scars.

—Judy T. Burnette,
former advocate manager for CASA

God promises us in Jeremiah that He will satisfy the weary and bring joy to those who sorrow. *Beyond the Scars* is a living testament to the healing capacity of trust, faithfulness, and forgiveness. Collier creates a space in her soul where readers can witness the transformative power of God as she experiences deliverance from complex trauma to strength and resiliency.

—Monica W. Lones, MA, MEd

I highly recommend this book for any person or family member affected by substance abuse and/or physical or mental abuse at any age. The personal journey of the author gives us an authentic account of her life struggles and her personal victory over evil. She reconnects with the Creator whom she knew as a child and whom she thought had abandoned her on many occasions only to find He never did. She discovers forgiveness to be the path to loving herself and others.

—Phyllis C. Everett, MSN, RN, AOCN, NP-C

I too have lived a trauma-filled life. Although Amy's trauma is horrible to read, she has allowed God's constant presence in her life to break those dysfunctional cycles that no one before her was ever brave enough to tackle. Such a great resource to help other women who have been silenced and oppressed to speak up. Knowing Amy's heart for children, as we served in CASA of Central Virginia together, I see this book is another tool to help parents and children realize what could be taking place in silence.

—Kelly Hahn, former CASA advocate

Raw and emotional! *Beyond the Scars* is a story of resilience, hope, and healing. This intense memoir takes you on a journey of learning to forgive, recognizing your self-worth, and realizing even in our darkest moments that God is with us.

—Karen Amato,
an executive director in
early childhood education

For anyone who has suffered domestic abuse and lost faith in God, this story is for you. If you are someone in doubt of hope, faith, or survival of a domestic abuse relationship, this is a must-read. The compassion, honesty, and strong will of this author's story demonstrates that domestic violence is real and that there is hope for you. If you want to learn how to overcome and see God's light read this book. The author has articulated abuse in great detail and demonstrates a story of strong will and faith to survive it. It's a heartfelt story to never lose hope and to believe in redemption and the transformative power of God.

—Melissa S. Meador,
Human Resources Manager,
former VA Social Services Benefits Program Specialist

WOW! *Beyond the Scars* is a must-read! A journey through rejection, abuse, grief, and disappointments. I couldn't stop reading. God never leaves us through the pain. You're still a daughter of the King!

—Helen K. Walters, business owner

Amy Collier shares a glimpse of her heartbreak, anger, guilt, and search for answers in *Beyond the Scars*. Amy's life story unveils a strong, caring, remarkable woman who has survived many forms of abuse. Her story tells how difficult it is to let go and trust in God. Through reading, you will discover the angels who entered her life. Hopefully, by reading Amy's story, discussions will develop that aid others to seek help and not feel so very alone.

—Julia V. Robertson,
retired school teacher

A painful story of struggle and heartbreak, sadly shared by many. I am grateful for your courage to share with us the reminder that God is always with us even when we don't feel like it sometimes. May God continue to strengthen you.

—Deborah McCoy, lifelong friend

Beyond the Scars

HOW I LEARNED GOD DIDN'T
ABANDON ME IN MY DARKEST HOUR

AMY K. COLLIER

Birmingham, Alabama

Beyond the Scars

Iron Stream
An imprint of Iron Stream Media
100 Missionary Ridge
Birmingham, AL 35242
IronStreamMedia.com

Library of Congress Control Number: 2022950704

Cover design by Hannah Linder Designs

ISBN: 978-1-56309-619-8 (paperback)
ISBN: 978-1-56309-620-4 (eBook)

1 2 3 4 5—27 26 25 24 23

This book is dedicated to
my husband, Charlie,
and
my three wonderful children
Cindy, Dustin, and Charles.
Thank you for your love and support.

Author's Note

The events and conversations in this book have been reconstructed to the best of my recollection, how I remembered it along with the use of my journals. Others may have their own or different views or memories of the same event. Some names and details have been changed to protect the identity of both the innocent and the guilty. It is my hope that by sharing my story others can find hope, healing, strength, and inspiration.

Contents

Prologue

To be completely honest with you and with myself, I should not be here. Only by the grace of God have I survived. It is simply a miracle that the types of drugs and large quantities I put into my body time and time again did not end my life or cause lasting effects to my overall health.

I believe without any doubts I survived only because I was meant to share my story. Not only to bring awareness to abuse but also to reach others who have suffered from some form of abuse at some point and time in their lives. It is even more important to bring awareness to the effect abuse has on one's life, the scars it leaves behind, and how those scars influence the decisions we make for the rest of our lives. The effects of the abuse I suffered affected the lives of the people who are the closest to me. I want to share how victims can go from being prisoners of their pasts to jailers of their minds.

To say my faith was tried, tested, and pushed to the limits is an understatement. I was brought up to believe God loved His children and protected them. As a believer, I questioned His love, His existence, and everything I was taught with the onset of the abuse. I couldn't help but question. Wasn't I a child of God? Why was I not worthy of His love and protection?

In times of trauma and tragedy, you either run to or from God. I was the latter. I not only ran from Him; I blamed Him.

Day by day, week by week, year by year, time passed, and then one day something happened and forced me to wake up from the fog that had become a way of life. I looked at the broken pieces and realized I was lost and tired of hurting and pushing people away. I wanted to break the cycle of torment, but how?

It was only after putting my story to paper that I could see how all the broken pieces fit together and in doing so I could begin to heal.

I now understood . . .

I would no longer allow emotional, physical, or sexual abuse to define who I am as a person. I'm so much more. I was never alone no matter how lonely I felt or how hard I tried to push God away. Despite the horrible things I said to Him, He never left my side. No matter how broken, the pieces of my life could still be put together even if it did take twenty-six years.

I realized the abuse I endured was *not* my fault. So much of my life had been stolen from me. I hated myself because of the shame I felt. As the years of self-loathing went by, I became my own worst enemy and my next abuser.

I'm going to share a story of how I—a thirty-seven-year-old mother of three at the time—ended up on the bathroom floor, broken, bleeding, and lost, convinced there was no such thing as a life beyond the scars I carried and how those scars ruined lives— not just my own. Once I recognized the destruction, I realized a broken life and a broken family can alter the cycle of a way of life for future generations.

The power of your mind can make or break you. Allow me to share with you the power of faith.

In this journey we are about to take together, I want you to know you are not alone. I desire for you to be inspired, to have a new sense of hope, and to allow yourself to find a way out of the darkness. It's time to begin a brand-new life. You are worthy! Something good can come out of something bad. There is strength buried deep inside all of us. Come with me and see how I found peace among the brokenness and the scars.

This is my life Beyond the Scars.

CHAPTER 1

From Prisoner to Jailer

I sat on the bathroom floor with my forehead resting on top of my knees, hugging my legs close to my chest, and cried uncontrollable tears as the pain and hurt consumed me. I could no longer pretend to be okay; I was far from okay. The will to fight for a life of peace and happiness beyond the scars, that deep down in my soul I never believed I deserved, left me.

I know what I must do. I can't take it anymore. I'm too emotionally exhausted and weak to fight it any longer; it is the only way I know to make the recordings in my mind stop. I stood up, wiped my face, and blew my nose. Taking a deep breath, I opened the bathroom door and walked toward the kitchen on a mission, the same mission I'd been on many times over the past twenty-six years.

As I entered the dimly lit kitchen, I searched for the sharpest knife I owned; the one my father had given me years earlier. I couldn't wake up the boys or it would mess up everything.

"Please don't wake up, please don't wake up," I silently repeated over and over. There it was in front of me, the fillet knife from my father. A sense of accomplishment rushed over me. The blade would save me from the pain I could no longer tolerate. I ran my finger across the thin edge, feeling the sharpness.

Yes, this will work.

I wrapped the knife inside a kitchen towel. If one of the boys woke up and entered the kitchen, he wouldn't know what I was about to do. Sweat ran down my sides and my heart pounded faster. There was no turning back. I held the concealed knife, walked back into the bathroom, and locked the door behind me. I took a deep breath, grateful I had made it back to privacy with no interruptions. I caught a glimpse of myself in the mirror. My swollen eyes and tear-streaked face stared back at me. My thoughts raced, accompanied by the pounding of my heart. The relentless negative recordings played.

Just look at you. What the hell are you doing? Are you really this weak?

I wanted to be stronger. I wanted the recordings to stop.

Just look at yourself. I hate you. You deserve to hurt. You deserve to bleed. You push everybody away. You can't do anything right. Nobody loves you. You're all alone. You're worthless. Your kids deserve so much better than a broken mother like you.

Sobbing, I sank to the cold, hard floor and stared at the wrapped knife in my shaking hands. Defeated and broken, I no longer had the strength or will to fight my memories.

You win! You're right. I just want it to stop, it must stop! I deserve to bleed. I deserve to hurt.

My eyes remained on the kitchen towel clutched in my hands until my knuckles turned white. Unwrapping the cloth, I held the knife in my left hand and stared at my right wrist, repeating, "I hate you. You deserve this. You deserve to hurt. You deserve to bleed. You deserve all the pain that you feel."

I squeezed the knife tighter in my shaking hand, took a deep breath, and closed my eyes as the blade ran across my wrist. It burned, and the blood flowed. The blade in my hand felt like a part of me, becoming a replacement for the blood leaving my body.

I hate you. You deserve this. I hate you.

I could not see the extent of the damage through my tear-filled eyes, but deep inside I felt I deserved more physical pain. It wasn't enough yet.

With every ounce of anger I held deep down inside, I ran the blade across my wrist as hard as I physically could. I yelled out to God, my God, the one who was supposed to protect me, save me, but in my mind, He'd turned His back on me years ago.

"Where are you? Why won't you protect me from this pain? Why won't you help me? Why do you continue to punish me? Why won't you just let me die?"

I looked down at my wounds; my wrist was covered in blood. It ran down my forearm and dripped into a puddle on the floor, but I still felt the emotional pain. Still heard my self-loathing playing like an audio track on repeat. I had to make it stop. A panic rushed over me, and I again drove the fillet knife across my wrist, cutting through the already gushing blood. The burning and stinging were stronger.

As fast as the episode started, it ended. I took a deep breath. The tightness in my chest released as my focus shifted from the emotional to the physical pain. Numbness flowed through my body except for the burning of my bloody wrist. It was over. The voices stopped.

Had I tried to commit suicide or was it just another act of self-harm? I honestly don't know. All I knew was at that moment I experienced relief because of the break in the emotional pain. Maybe dying would have been a plus.

I jumped at the sound of my sixteen-year-old son, Dustin, knocking on the bathroom door.

"Mom, let me in, open this door," he demanded from the other side.

Little did I know the cutting on that night would lead me to a greater insight.

CHAPTER 2

The Middle of Nowhere

I have difficulty describing my childhood. I remember how I felt growing up, but most childhood memories are lost to me. My journals are the keys to unlocking those missing years. I tread lightly retrieving my past, fearing painful flashbacks might be triggered.

To understand me and how I ended up bleeding on the bathroom floor, I need to go back to the dynamics of my family, which was the epitome of dysfunction.

My family consisted of my dad, mom, brother, two sisters, and me. My brother, Brian, is six years older than me, my sister Lisa is four years older, and Angela, the baby, is two years younger. I never called her by her real name. *Angela* sounded funny to me. Brian gave her the nickname Pudding when she was an infant, and later we shortened it to Puddy. She still goes by this name.

Our family of six had briefly been a family of seven. Another sibling—Brandon—was born two years before me in November 1970.

"He passed away twelve hours after his birth," Mom told me.

Brandon died from infant respiratory distress syndrome, previously called hyaline membrane syndrome.

"I was too medicated to go to his funeral. No one allowed me to say goodbye. He was *my* son." Forty-four years later Mom's words still carry resentment and anger from not being allowed to say goodbye. Sometimes I wonder if, in losing my brother, Mom lost a part of herself.

As a teenager I would sit in my room and talk to Brandon whenever I felt lonely. I imagined what he looked like and wondered how different life would have been if he hadn't passed away. I pretended we were best friends, and somehow, I didn't feel so alone. I wanted desperately to feel loved by a family member. Why not a brother in heaven who I never met?

I didn't know my extended family well because we visited so infrequently. I could walk past most of them on the street and not even know it. This was before the internet and social media.

During the process of writing this book, I asked my mom to tell me what her dad and mom were like. I wanted an idea about her childhood, which was something she never talked about. I hoped to understand her better. Mom was born and raised in Delaware; her two brothers and two sisters remained there, and we would visit them once a year. During my teenage years the visits stopped.

"Mama didn't hug or give kisses," Mom said. "She seemed distant and, I don't know, maybe depressed."

Interestingly, this is the same way I would describe my mother. Could this unhealthy family cycle be broken?

She continued, "Daddy spoiled me but was very strict with the others. Maybe it was because I was so sick as a child."

At age eight my mom fell ill with rheumatic fever. She was bedridden for two years. Rheumatic fever is an inflammatory disease that can develop as a complication of inadequately treating strep throat or scarlet fever. Mom's sickness affected her heart. During the years of her illness, my mom would let her mother know she was awake by grabbing the broom handle from beside her bed and tapping the floor. My grandmother would carry her downstairs to a bed set up in the living room. Mom did not see her mother for the rest of the day. She spent her days alone, drawing and coloring in bed.

Growing up I was in awe of my mom's talent as an artist. I tried to mimic the way she blended and shaded colors in her pictures. I didn't know she was self-taught.

Every three months her dad took her to the doctor for blood work, and afterward they stopped for ice cream. My grandfather liked Neapolitan, and Mom liked vanilla. Her mom never went with them to the doctor's office and never joined them for ice cream.

My father grew up on a beef and dairy farm in Pennsylvania with his dad, mom, and three brothers. Every morning and after school the sons had their chores, and my father was responsible for the care of 125 pigs. He woke up at 4:00 a.m., worked the farm, went to school, returned, did household chores, worked the farm again, ate dinner, did homework, and went to bed. Dad has always worked very hard. I admire and respect that about him.

"Mom was strict; she didn't show much affection," Dad told me. Again, I saw the same pattern with my father's mother as with my mother's mother. Could the relationship with their mother have been a factor as to why all four boys in my father's family joined branches of the service immediately after graduating high school? Were they trying to get away from home?

At one point in my childhood, my father's youngest brother lived across the street from us, before he moved to Texas. I only have one memory of him living so close. On a Saturday morning my younger sister and I laid on the couch in the living room watching cartoons. My dad and his brother argued, then my uncle unplugged the television and carried it out the front door. My sister and I cried. Without saying a word, Dad left the house, slamming the door behind him, and went to work. My sister and I were never told what happened. Even as an adult, I have no idea why my uncle took the television.

My dad's mom lived close by for nearly four years. My siblings and I spent more time around her than around any other relative except our parents. One time I was at her house and hurt myself by tripping over a tree stump. I ran inside crying. Instead of comforting me she said, "Stop crying. If it isn't bleeding, it doesn't hurt." Then she put me to work. She always had plenty of chores for us to do. I was around eight when she moved to Georgia to be closer to another son and his family. We went to visit her when I was eleven, and I didn't see her again until thirteen years later.

I'm not sure she ever smiled. There were never any hugs, kisses, or I love yous. My grandmother talked negatively about my mom, which made me feel uncomfortable and sometimes angry. She loved to talk about how wonderful she thought our cousins were and how they did better in school. I never once heard her say she was proud of anyone in my family. I was not good enough in her eyes. When I was fourteen, she let me know in a letter how true that was.

After talking with my parents and recalling some memories, I realized why I never felt loved or like I measured up to my parents' or my grandparents' expectations. My parents did love me but didn't know how to show love. I firmly believe and have said many times, "People learned how they live."

In 1976, my family left Delaware and moved eight hours away to a small Virginia town to start a mushroom farm. My dad's mushroom farm was the only one in the state, and he was proud to say so. He worked from sunup to sundown to make his business successful. I rode on the back of the tractor just to spend time with him. A lot of my childhood was spent helping around the mushroom house.

Mom, on the other hand, cried every day for a year for being—in her words—ripped away from her home and family. I was too young to remember the move, but I wonder how it affected my older brother and sister, who had to leave all their friends to move to the middle of nowhere and witness Mom's extreme unhappiness.

My mother was a stay-at-home mom and very strict. She didn't show us affection and was easily angered. She would pick up the closest thing within her reach to hit us. I grew afraid of making her mad, which didn't take much.

My sisters and I were sometimes locked out of the house for her to have *alone* time. Usually, she was not alone. Often, the same person visited when Dad was out delivering mushrooms. We never told our father anything. My siblings and I knew our mom's visitations were wrong. Once when we were locked outside, Puddy and I headed to play in the shed. As I opened the wooden door the wind caused it to fly open and slam into the back of Puddy's head. Blood seeped through her long, blonde hair. My older sister, Lisa, heard her crying and came running. She calmed Puddy down, then Lisa broke into the back door of our trailer, and the three of us crept into the bathroom to wash the blood out of Puddy's hair. We were careful not to disturb Mom's alone time.

During my teenage years, Mom changed. One minute she hit us if she thought we'd done something wrong. The next minute it didn't matter what we'd done or said. She acted like we no longer existed. My life filled with a sense of loss and confusion.

CHAPTER 3

Loss of My Innocence

At thirteen, I stopped trusting people and refused to allow others into my world. Tears, despair, and secrets filled my life as I learned to be silent and afraid.

I'd spent my childhood as a tomboy. I liked to get dirty as well as hunt and fish with my dad.

He often said, "This is the last time you're coming with me because you talk too much."

I nodded as I carried the tackle box and Dad balanced the fishing rods on his shoulder. We both knew I'd be by his side on the next outing. If he wasn't working or sleeping, he was hunting or fishing, and I jumped at every opportunity to be with him.

Our farm—along with mushrooms—consisted of horses, chickens, rabbits, dogs, cats, and a talking bird. I spent a lot of time riding horses and playing in the woods building forts. My little sister and I ventured outside in the mornings after fixing ourselves bowls of cereal and didn't return until dark. I loved staying busy, and I'm still like that today.

I also loved making people laugh.

"You knew no strangers," Mom said. "Even as a small child. You'd walk up and talk to anyone, smiling the whole time, as if you'd known them forever. You were always laughing."

The laughter stopped in 1985 when my innocence was ripped away from me.

My best friend Tom lived about a fifteen-minute walk from me. We spent a lot of time together and acted like brother and sister, but without sibling rivalry. During 1985 we were together most of the time. Even though he was a little more than a year older he didn't mind my company. One winter he shot me below my butt cheek with my own BB gun while we walked through the field.

"I was aiming for a bird." He gave me a mischievous smile.

"Oh, yeah," I chased him all the way to his house. He laughed when I stopped every few minutes to grab a handful of snow to hold to my wound.

"Next time it'll be you who gets shot," I said, laughing. I grabbed my BB gun from him as we entered his house. The laughter stopped when Tom's father looked at me. My uncomfortableness around Mr. Johnson grew. I tried to spend very little time around him, but as Tom and I hung out more at his place, avoiding his dad proved to be a challenge.

Mr. Johnson watched me when I entered a room. Even when I didn't see him do this, I felt his eyes on me. Often, he stared at my developing body and smirked. His expression caused my stomach to turn and the hairs on the back of my neck to stand up. He constantly glared and smirked at me. I avoided eye contact as much as possible and pretended he didn't scare me. But he did.

Since Tom's family didn't own a telephone, I would walk to his house, taking a chance he'd be home. Sometimes he wasn't. On one such occasion, his dad touched me for the first time, but it wouldn't be the last.

As I walked toward the front door Mr. Johnson approached from the side of the house.

"Is Tom here?" I shifted from one foot to the other, looking around for any sign of my friend.

His dad walked toward me, wiping his hands on a greasy rag. "You sure are pretty. I like those tight pants you're wearing." He tossed the rag and walked closer.

My heart raced. Everything inside me said run. I took a step back, but Mr. Johnson cornered me, then kissed me. The more I resisted, the tighter he held me in place and continued to shove his tongue into my mouth. Somehow, I freed myself and ran. When I was out of sight, I sat in a grassy field to catch my breath, placed my head in my hands, and cried. *What just happened?* When my sobs turned into quiet whimpers, I still felt the lingering taste of his tongue in my mouth. I scrubbed my lips and tongue with the back of my hand.

I decided not to tell anyone.

Over the next nine months he grew more aggressive. At first, he stared at me but turned his head when someone noticed. I'd hoped Tom would recognize my discomfort around his dad, but he didn't seem to. Soon Mr. Johnson stared at me no matter who saw him.

On another occasion when I visited Tom's brother, John, and his girlfriend, Mr. Johnson cornered me again. As I opened the back door, he grabbed me from behind and pinned me against the house. He leaned in to kiss me. I squirmed.

"John's inside waiting for me," I managed to choke out.

He turned his head as if to listen, then looked back at me and raised one corner of his mouth. When he let me go, I hurried inside and tried to keep my legs from buckling. I rarely visited their house after that, but one time when I did, it turned out to be a huge mistake.

Tom's mom had asked me to spend the night and babysit her infant niece while she and her husband headed to work the next day. I agreed because I knew Tom and John would be there. That night I slept in Tom's bedroom, and he and John slept in the bedroom at the other end of the house.

Mrs. Johnson woke me early the next morning.

"Amy," her quiet voice caused me to stir. "My husband isn't going to work. He's not feeling well, so he'll stay with the baby. You can head home once you're up." She left the room, closing the door behind her.

It was still dark outside when Mrs. Johnson's car pulled out of the driveway. I yawned and fell back asleep. The next thing I knew, Mr. Johnson was on top of me. The weight of his body pinned me down as he touched me under my nightgown with his hand hot against my flesh.

My heartbeat sounded in my ears as I struggled to breathe.

He grabbed my face and forced me to look at him. "Keep your mouth shut and don't make a sound. Understand?"

I nodded and prayed over and over for God to please save me.

Mr. Johnson's stale breath assaulted my face and neck. I wanted to throw up. Tears fell past my temples and onto the pillow.

God, please.

The baby in the other room cried.

Mr. Johnson swore but rolled off me and headed to the door. He turned. "Got to quiet the baby before she wakes the boys." He glared at me. "Don't move. I'll be right back."

I got up when I no longer heard him outside of the room. I adjusted my underwear and nightgown then approached the door and peeked out. The sounds coming from the kitchen confirmed he was preparing a bottle. I ran down the hall into the bedroom where Tom and John slept.

I shook Tom. "Wake up, please, wake up."

He mumbled something.

"Tom!" I glanced at the door. My body trembled.

John rolled over and opened his eyes. "Amy? Are you okay?" He sat up.

I opened my mouth to say something, but John shifted his eyes toward the bedroom door. My heart stopped as I felt his dad's glare burn on my back. I looked over my shoulder. Mr. Johnson stood in the doorway and stared at me with such fury I took a step back. He stood there for what seemed like an eternity, never saying a word, the silence deafening. Finally, he turned and walked away.

"Amy?" John raised his brow.

"Tom, wake up. I want to go home." Tears filled my eyes as I shook him.

John punched his brother in the shoulder.

Tom jerked awake, swore at John, and then noticed me. "Amy?"

I crossed my arms, but it did very little to stop my violent shaking. I whispered, "I want to go home."

"Now?"

John punched him again.

"Stop." Tom shoved his brother, then swung his legs to the side of the bed. "Okay."

I made him promise to wait outside the bedroom while I changed out of my nightgown and dressed. Tom walked me to the edge of the yard. As he turned to go back inside, I ran.

Once out of sight of the Johnsons' place I dropped to my knees in my familiar spot in the field and cried until my ribs ached. When my tears stopped, I stood and, with a heavy sigh, headed home. I wrestled with so many questions along the way. Would my parents believe me if I told them? What if they blamed me? Would they keep me from seeing my friend?

When I entered the house, I wanted nothing more than to head to my room, but my older sister, Lisa, stopped me. "You've been crying, what happened?"

I looked away, determined not to tell her of the nightmare I'd experienced.

She grabbed my arm and pulled me down the hall into her bedroom. Once she'd closed the door, Lisa turned toward me. "Well?"

I shook my head, unable to prevent the tears from flowing down my cheeks again.

"You're not leaving this room until you tell me what's going on." She crossed her arms.

"You can't tell anyone." I gripped her shoulders. "Promise."

She nodded. We sat on her bed, and I told her everything. Lisa was angry, but surprisingly not at me like I'd imagined. She wrapped her arm around my shoulders and leaned her cheek against the top of my head. We sat for a while in silence. I had no more words to say, and I don't think Lisa knew what to say. I left her and went to my room.

The next day, Mom yelled for me to join her outside. I found my parents sitting on lawn chairs, both looking uncomfortable.

"Lisa told us everything." Mom held my gaze.

So much for keeping a promise. Anger and betrayal rose in me but so did relief because I no longer needed to keep my secret.

"You can't tell anyone. No one would believe you if you did." Mom folded her hands in her lap.

I opened my mouth in shock and looked at Dad.

Mom continued, "This would hurt your father's mushroom business."

Dad cleared his throat. "His niece said something similar. It went to court, but nobody believed her. Do you think they'll believe you?"

Instead of protecting me, they abandoned me. A slap across the face would have been less painful. My parents placed the business and their reputation over my need for them to keep me safe. A grown man in our neighborhood molested me, their thirteen-year-old daughter, and they wanted us all to keep silent. Without responding, I turned and headed back to my room.

Lisa came to my bedroom later and told me she was sorry, but she believed our parents needed to know.

I snapped at her, "Like anybody cares."

I told how our parents reacted, and she stormed out of the room, slamming the door behind her. She was angry at them for not doing anything. My anger still simmered toward her because she'd told in the first place.

The incident was never mentioned again, and this was the first of many lessons I learned about keeping secrets. As an adult, I brought it up with my mom and shared how hurt I felt toward her and Dad for not protecting me. She denied being told about what Mr. Johnson had done. I dropped the conversation. Mom was the master at pretending painful memories of my childhood never existed.

To this day I believe John had an idea of what his dad had done, because afterward when I visited, he made sure I wasn't alone with his father. If Mr. Johnson walked into a room, John found a reason to get me out. I often wondered what went through John's mind when his father had stood in the doorway and he witnessed the awkward silence, the anger on his father's face, and the urgency for me to get out of the house. I don't know if Tom and John talked about the strangeness of the morning when everything happened. I do know the dynamics of my relationship with Tom changed. Our friendship was never the same.

That morning may have been the last time Mr. Johnson touched me, but he continued to play emotional head games with me many years later as an adult. There were times I ran into him at the local convenience store. He'd watched me with the same smirk on his face I remembered as a child. He looked pleased with the fear and uneasiness he caused. I hated him, not only for the innocence he'd stolen from me or the pain, fear, and shame he caused but because he seemed to take pride in what he'd done and gotten away with.

I lived in a very small town where everyone knew everybody, and secrets weren't kept forever. Later in life I discovered there were others whose lives he had destroyed.

At a young age, I learned scars and secrets go hand in hand. Soon depression took over my life along with suicidal thoughts.

CHAPTER 4

The Shed

S creaming in my house was the norm. Crying—one of the few ways I dealt with the stress—was my curse.

"Are you crying again?" my brother said after another shouting match with my sister. "You're such a cry baby," he said inches from my face.

Mom reprimanded me whenever I cried, then continued her rant at Dad or anyone else present. Hiding in my room with my hands over my ears could not silence the yelling throughout the house. The place I called home turned into a battlefield where six miserable people lived inside a very small trailer. Anger and hate filled every room. I desperately wanted to wake up from the nightmare of my life. At thirteen, I'd lost my innocence and my security of being safe. Now I was on my way to losing my family to destructive ways. I needed to find a way out. My solution almost gave me a permanent way out.

"Dad." I inched closer to the recliner on a day when a truce resided in the house. Mom had been gone since the day before—an occurrence that had increased in frequency. Music sounded from my brother's room, and Lisa remained in hers. The smell of Dad's last cigarette lingered.

"What?" He reached for another one.

"I want to move out."

He snorted at my request. Before he could call me a fool or any other choice words he had in mind, I continued. "Just to the shed. I want to move into the shed." I looked away. What if he said no?

He sighed. "Do what you want."

Dad didn't care what I did, or he lacked the strength to argue. His business faced the threat of bankruptcy, and Mom was gone all the time. The following weekend Dad and I took most of the boxes Mom stored in the shed to the mushroom house. My bed and dresser scraped across the concrete floor as we put them in place. Dad held my gaze when we were done then shook his head. Without a word he headed back to the house. I finally had a place to call my own away from the strife.

The shed—a ten-by-ten square building made of gray cinder-block with a tin roof—sat in the woods behind our trailer. A light bulb hung from the ceiling, and a large chest freezer took up the wall on the right side. The boxes Mom wouldn't allow Dad and me to move remained on top of the freezer.

Inside, my bed and dresser were to the left with enough space in the center of the room for an electric portable heater. It smelled of old mildewed clothes and mothballs. The tall wooden door at the front of the shed, warped from the weather, was difficult to open. I had to grip the handle and repeatedly pull and push until it wiggled open. The scraping of the door on the concrete floor almost sounded like a wounded animal. A fitting sound for a wounded teenager.

Along the length of the door top, an inch-wide opening allowed light to shine in. The beam originated from a pole outside, which remained on from dusk to dawn. I welcomed the light; I no longer liked the dark. Darkness represented places where little girls were hurt. The crack allowed the light to enter as well as the cold. At night my teeth chattered as my breath floated into the air. Fully dressed and under the covers, I'd curl into a ball trying to keep warm, the electric heater pulled as close to my bed as possible. I'd stare at the red coil while the motor hummed, holding out my freezing hands until they nearly touched the metal guard. Numbness filled my fingers, and I doubted my hands would ever thaw. Eventually, I'd pull the covers over my head and wait for sleep to overtake my trembling body. Ah, yes, my sanctuary. My lonely, dark, freezing paradise.

The shed protected me against the toxic environment in the house, but it did not protect me against loneliness. I had the freedom to cry, but the bondage of depression grew tighter around me. No one knew I spent hours crying in that very cold place. No one checked on me to see if I was okay. No one cared if I froze to death. So why should I have cared if I died from the cold or by my own hands?

While staying in the shed with winter in full force, I had no desire to live. It didn't matter I was only thirteen. One day I took one of my dad's hunting knives out of his gun cabinet and hid it under my pillow. Not wanting someone to find me too soon, I planned to wait until everyone was asleep to carry out my plan. When nightfall came, I sat in my bed and wrote what I believed would be my last entry in my journal. I took the knife from under my pillow, took a deep breath, and pushed the tip against my wrist and pulled downward. Warm blood flowed over my skin, and a stinging and burning sensation overcame me. Committing suicide was my intent, but the wound had not been deep enough to kill me. However, the racing thoughts in my mind stopped, and my focus shifted to the physical pain. Both surprised and satisfied with my new discovery, I'd found a way to stop the emotional hurt. I retrieved a long sock from my dresser and wrapped it around my wrist to stop the bleeding. With the knife back under my pillow, I climbed into bed. My wrist continued to burn with every movement, but I welcomed the pain because of the sense of relief it gave me.

A couple months shy of fourteen I entered the eighth grade where cigarettes, pot, pills, and drinking became a regular part of my life. I proceeded to get kicked out of school for fighting and arrested for possession of marijuana—which wasn't mine but one of my friend's. The school called my dad. He watched with indifference as a police officer read me my rights. I usually never faced consequences for acting out. My actions screamed for someone to notice me, to see the self-destructive path I'd chosen. Why couldn't they see that the quiet little girl who used to bend over backward to make everybody smile had disappeared? My mom, who used to beat me over nothing, turned into a parent who acted like I didn't exist. I'd rather have been beaten, at least then I would know Mom cared enough to punish me. I needed my parents to care, but there seemed to be nothing I could do severe enough to get their attention.

Believe me, I tried. One such occasion happened the day of a football game during my ninth-grade year.

"Why weren't you at school today?" Mom stood in the doorway blocking my path. She folded her arms but still managed to raise her cigarette to her mouth. "Heard you and Sammy skipped."

Mom never confronted me about my behavior. "Yeah." I chewed my lower lip.

She blew smoke over my head. "You're grounded." My mom turned and entered the house.

"What?" I followed. "The football game's tonight. I want to go."

She faced me again, one hand on her hip while pointing the cigarette at me with the other. "Home by ten."

I nodded.

In the evening, Mom dropped Sammy and me off at school. Students headed into the stadium, and I caught a whiff of concession stand food. We headed in the direction of the entrance.

"Home by ten," Mom called after me.

I responded over my shoulder. "I heard you." Sammy and I had no intention of going to the game. Instead, we waited for her boyfriend. When he arrived, we rode around in his car, drinking and getting high. At midnight, two hours past my curfew, I stumbled to my parents' bedroom reeking of alcohol and weed. Mom woke up when I fell on the floor next to her side of the bed.

"It's midnight," I slurred.

"So what? Don't you dare puke in here."

Somehow, I made it to the bathroom before I threw up, then collapsed in front of the toilet. The coolness of the laminated floor helped with the nausea. The next morning, I woke cold and shivering with the smell of vomit on my clothes. I squinted against the sunlight. I had never made it to the shed the previous night but had fallen asleep in the front yard. My mouth felt dry but tasted worse. A headache pounded behind my eyes and my body screamed against the stiffness as I stood. I took a few stumbling steps toward the shed.

"Amy," Mom yelled from the front door. "Why the hell did you wake me up last night?"

I squinted in her direction, unable to form an answer.

She huffed before slamming the door.

I stood there alone as my world continued to shatter. In less than a year, I'd been molested, used drugs, been arrested, and been drunk enough to collapse in the front yard. All before I turned fourteen. My mom had lost her sweet little girl, and it didn't seem to bother her. Would it bother her if I died?

January 1986, several weeks after I turned fourteen, a friend gave me a brown grocery bag half full of prescription bottles to keep for them. I hid the drugs in the shed, but as my life continued to spiral downward, I saw the pills as a way to escape. Determined to take enough to end my life, I swallowed a variety of prescription drugs until I couldn't swallow any more. I left no note. Why would I if I didn't believe my family cared what I thought or felt? In my bed, I drifted in and out of consciousness. Then I heard a voice; I truly believe it was God's.

Your work is not complete, and you must go back.

I don't know how long I was unconscious, but when I woke the words continued to play in my mind. I clenched my teeth and my fists. "How dare you, God." I rushed outside and threw up. For two weeks I'd go from the couch to the bathroom. I couldn't move without getting sick. My life existed of throwing up or sleeping. It's amazing how much someone can vomit without eating. On January 28, 1986, I laid on the couch, afraid to move from nausea, and watched the Space Shuttle Challenger lift off and explode over the Atlantic Ocean. I raged inside. *God, how could you let those seven innocent people lose their lives? I want to die, yet you won't let me. It's not fair.*

I yelled at God, "You said my work is not complete. Are you kidding? What work? My pain and suffering? What more is there? What do you want from me?"

Was I being punished? Why?

Before everything had happened, I had attended church every week. My family didn't go, but I was fortunate enough to live beside two preachers from different churches. On Wednesdays and Sundays, I would catch a ride to church with one of them and his family. Most of the time, I went to church three times a week. Around age eleven I was baptized. I loved God, and I wanted nothing more than to devote my life to Him. No one in my family came for my special day.

After Mr. Johnson's advances and inappropriate touching, I stopped going to church and turned my anger toward God. I believed He'd turned His back on me, and I wasn't good enough for His love, just as I believed I wasn't good enough to be loved by my family.

No one knew I had tried to take my life. Mom thought I had the flu, but by the second week of my illness she decided I had a sinus infection. Since she didn't believe in doctors, I was relieved no one ever found out my second attempt to end my life had failed.

CHAPTER 5

You Can't Save Me

During the next six months I tried to end my life four times. I never told anyone and never left a note. My home life continued to be a nightmare. The childhood I knew no longer existed and caused my despair to increase every day.

At school, I often stopped in front of the guidance counselor's office trying to force myself to go inside. I desperately wanted someone to tell me everything would be okay, but I allowed fear, shame, and guilt to keep me away. *What if they don't believe me or blame me for what's happened?* I blamed myself enough; I didn't need someone else to do so as well.

One morning, I opened up to my friend Jessica as we headed down the hallway to our next class.

"I wish I were dead," I said.

"What?" Jessica glanced at me. "You don't mean that."

When I didn't respond, neither did she. The next thing I knew I was asked to go to the guidance counselor's office. I looked over at Jessica and she mouthed, *I'm sorry.* As I headed to the office, I struggled with what to say. I had two choices: lie and say I didn't mean it or tell the truth. In my experience nothing good came from telling the truth.

I entered the office where two chairs sat on one side of the desk and my counselor sat on the other. I glanced around the room trying to look anywhere else but at her. I swallowed.

"Have a seat," she said.

I did so without looking up.

"Amy, do you want to talk?" Concern filled her voice.

When I did raise my eyes to meet hers, I burst into tears. Through sobs I said I wanted to die and had attempted to kill myself on several occasions. What I didn't share was how furious I was to be alive or how much pain I carried. I didn't tell her how my best friend's dad had molested me or how much my family was falling apart. Deep down I believed all the anger in my home was my fault. My parents had embedded in me whatever happened in the Kunkle house stayed in the Kunkle house.

Finding out I wanted to die and had attempted suicide made matters worse. The guidance counselor called my parents and made an appointment for me to speak with a child psychologist the same day. After school I waited outside for Mom to pick me up. Little if any conversation took place on the ride home. I preferred the silence over the awkwardness of trying to talk anyway.

Because I'd opened my mouth, Jessica, the guidance counselor, the child psychologist, and—worst of all—my parents knew of my desire to die. I didn't direct my anger toward Jessica because I knew she was worried, but opening up to her had caused me to be placed on a waiting list to be hospitalized. My parents and siblings were furious with me, but not as angry as I was with myself. For two weeks, while I waited to go to the hospital, I received the silent treatment from my family. I would have given anything to hear my mom or dad say "I love you" or "I just want you to get better" or "we'll get through this." Those words never came.

During the four-hour drive to Richmond, I sat in the back seat of the car and silently cried. Dad gripped the steering wheel and shouted over the seat at me. I felt like he was ashamed of me and was afraid of what everyone would think of me being in a mental hospital. Mom's silence showed she agreed with him.

I tried to take a deep breath then pressed my fist into my mouth to keep from sobbing out loud. Attempting to drown out his words—*disappointed, embarrassed, ashamed*—I stared out the window. Why didn't he add *completely worthless?* At one point in my life, I thought my dad walked on water, but the hateful words he said that day ripped through my heart and soul. My father's anger and disappointment in me caused more emotional damage than anything else and would influence the decisions I'd make over the next twelve years.

By the time we arrived at the hospital I'd completely shut down—feeling beyond broken and beyond repair. A tall fence with rows of barbed wire rested around the top of the building. The sight terrified me. Was this a hospital or a prison? My father exited the car and slammed the door. He headed toward the entrance with Mom. Neither looked at or spoke to me. What was the point of being there if they treated me as if getting better wasn't worth it?

A nurse led us to an elevator, and when we arrived at the fourth floor, she pulled a set of keys from her pocket and proceeded to unlock each door we passed through. Each locked door told me I couldn't escape. We entered a large open room with several couches and a TV in the center. The nurses' station in the back area was surrounded by glass windows and another locked door. She must have noticed me staring in that direction.

"We want to be able to see the patients because we don't want anyone to try and hurt themselves." She looked at me.

I folded my arms behind my back to hide the scars. Shared bedrooms were along two sides of the room. The bathrooms and showers on the other wall reminded me of the girls' locker room at school. The boys stayed on a different hall.

"I'll show you to your room."

I took a final glance around the room before I fell into step behind her and my parents. She opened the door to a sparsely furnished space with two beds.

"For the next few days, you'll have no contact with anyone outside of the hospital. This is done to allow you to adjust to your surroundings." The nurse spoke—what I assumed to be— rehearsed words. "I'll give you a few minutes to say goodbye." She offered my parents a weak smile, then one to me before she stepped out.

"Well?" Dad shoved his hands in his pants pockets and looked at Mom.

"Well, guess it's time to go." She returned his gaze. Neither looked at me.

I wanted to scream "Look at me, I'm here in front of you! Why are you leaving me here? Why can't you love me?" Instead, I stared at the bed I'd occupy for the next several weeks.

"Bye, Amy," Mom said. They turned and walked out.

The nurse returned, handed me my schedule, and explained the expectations.

Everything had a set time. When to get up, get dressed, go to breakfast, to class, to lunch, then back to class. Group therapy came after class followed by individual therapy—the only time we weren't with the entire group—then dinner, and finally back to our rooms. Prepare for bed by 9:00 p.m., lights out by 9:30. We also had designated phone time with limited minutes to talk. Telephone and TV privileges were taken away for violations of any rules. The rigorous schedule gave me little time alone, which meant less time to lie in bed and cry. The huge adjustment caused me to have trouble sleeping. Where I lived in the country, the sound of crickets had filled my nights, but at the hospital my sleep was interrupted with ambulance sirens and nurses doing room checks. On my second night I suffered an anxiety attack, but at the time I had no idea what was happening to me. I woke with severe chest pains. My parents were contacted and gave permission for me to be taken to the medical hospital where the doctor gave me something for the pain and to help me calm down. Anxiety became one more thing to add to my what's-wrong-with-Amy list.

As I made friends at the treatment center, I learned a key component of survival—keeping my mouth shut. Silence was more important than truth if I wanted my freedom. I believed I lived in an environment where I would be punished for saying how I really felt. Instead, I said what the medical team wanted to hear me say in hopes of getting out sooner. I planned to go home and kill myself at the first possible opportunity. With my death, I would no longer be the problem in my screwed-up family. I cried myself to sleep every night then smiled at my therapist the next day as though everything were okay.

My dad and siblings never visited, but Mom came once a week. She didn't come because she wanted to but thought the hospital expected her to. I felt a cold distance between us as we struggled to converse. A sense of worthlessness loomed over me with each visit.

One day when my friends and I watched TV, a nurse approached and held out an envelope.

"Amy, you've got a letter."

"A letter?" Receiving a letter was a rare occurrence, and I headed to my room so I could read it in private. My excitement grew with each step I took, and I smiled the whole way. Sitting on my bed, I stared at the envelope, amazed someone in my family— my grandmother—cared enough to write. My excitement quickly vanished after the greeting.

> *Amy,*
>
> *Your dad told me where you are, and I want you to know how disappointed I am. You should be ashamed of yourself. Do you know how much money your dad is paying to keep you there? There's nothing wrong with you except you've got the devil inside of you! How could you be so selfish? All you want is attention and you don't care about anyone else. You're an embarrassment for the entire family. I hope you're happy with yourself. Don't expect to hear from me again.*

Those were the last words my grandmother said to me for the next thirteen years.

I dropped the letter to the floor and gripped my hands in my lap until they hurt. I struggled to breathe as I closed my eyes and tilted my head toward the ceiling, letting the tears pour down my face. Why had I believed she would care when the rest of my family didn't? Her words echoed my father's: *disappointed, embarrassed, ashamed.*

Really, God? This is why you are keeping me alive?

I wanted to die more than I wanted to breathe. I ripped up the letter and cried in my room all night. When the nurses came to check on me, I pretended to be asleep. I didn't mention the letter to my therapist and continued to pretend everything was okay because I wanted to go home and finally end my life.

Initially, I had been told if I committed myself, my stay would only be two weeks, but if I didn't go voluntarily and had to go before a judge, my stay would be lengthened to a minimum of six weeks. I went voluntary, expecting to stay two weeks but was hospitalized for seven. The duration of my stay was yet another lie that added to my growing distrust of everyone.

Prior to being discharged, my doctor set up a meeting to discuss a family plan for returning home. I wanted to roll my eyes. Why? Did they have a plan for a family as messed up as mine? When I entered the therapist office, he sat in a chair opposite my mom with an empty one next to her. The doctor motioned for me to take the empty seat. My mother didn't acknowledge my presence. Where was my dad?

"We're here to discuss Amy's return—"

"Her dad and I are getting a divorce," Mom blurted out keeping her eyes on the doctor.

My stomach clenched so hard I wanted to throw up. *Was he leaving because of me? This was my fault.*

The doctor still believed I should return home for a trial run, but only for forty-eight hours.

When Mom pulled up to our trailer, Dad's truck was gone. It had been seven weeks since the horrible ride to the hospital, but I still missed him. Had I messed up so badly he didn't want to see me? Would I ever see my father again? Less than five minutes home and my heart already ached.

Mom and I exited the car. "Where's Dad?"

"He's staying at one of the other properties."

I headed to the front door and waited. "Which one?"

"The empty one. Why are you just standing there?" Mom pushed past me and entered the house, leaving me on the porch.

I'd grown so accustomed to locked doors at the hospital, I figured ours was too. I forgot we never locked doors. My emotions flip flopped between sadness and anger knowing Dad lived in a place with no furniture, electricity, or running water. Again, I questioned if he had left because of me.

My first night home, Mom went out. While I was in the hospital, Brian had moved into the shed, so I once again lived in the house. I laid in bed wide awake waiting to hear the door open and announce her return. Eventually I got up and headed to the living room. The clock showed 1:00 a.m. I paced until 1:30 then called every hospital within three counties, worried I'd find her at one of them. Later the next afternoon she strolled in and told me she'd gone home with someone she'd met at a bar. I balled my fists at my sides. I rather she'd been in one of the hospitals.

Forty-eight hours at home left me crushed and drained. Neither my mom nor dad spent any time with me during those two days. When I returned to Richmond, I headed to my room and cried myself to sleep. The thought of ever going home again paralyzed me with fear.

When I met with my doctor again, I wanted to scream. I wanted to tell him how my dad didn't want anything to do with me and my mom had stayed away the entire two days. I wanted to tell him how much it hurt, but I didn't. I fell back into the only way I knew to survive—I shut down and shut up. A week later my doctor released me. I left the treatment center understanding why some of my friends returned to the hospital more than once. Inside, we felt safe, protected from the world and the people who caused our pain. But without a support system in our outside worlds, we wouldn't be protected.

I'd been sent back to the source of my pain, with no protection and nowhere to hide.

CHAPTER 6

Abandoned

Not long after I returned home from the hospital, Mom and Dad legally separated, and two of my siblings left home as well. My brother moved to Delaware to live with our uncle, and my older sister moved to Georgia to live with our grandmother. Mom moved into town, only fifteen minutes away, and left me and my little sister with Dad. He filed for custody, and she didn't contest it. I felt unwanted, unloved, and abandoned by my mom. She never reached out to see if we were okay. My uncle—Mom's brother—did call.

"Don't expect to hear from your mom," he said. "She's started a new life. One that doesn't involve you girls."

At age fourteen and twelve we were truly abandoned by our mom. Yet, as teenagers, my little sister and I needed our mom more than ever.

My dad, who had worked from sunup to sundown my whole life, needed to figure out how to take care of us on his own. He was clueless about how to raise two teenage daughters. We moved to an old two-story house on the other side of town. My sister and I learned how to cook and wash clothes, and my dad learned how to go shopping. We did the best we could. Dad found a third-shift job, which meant my little sister and I were left alone at night. He placed a loaded .22-caliber pistol in a holster attached to one of his belts and hung it on my bed post before he left for work.

"Use this to protect you and your sister if someone breaks in," he said.

I'm pretty sure he didn't realize he'd given his severely depressed daughter who'd been hospitalized for several months for trying to commit suicide, a gun.

Each of us dealt with our sense of loss, fear, anger, and loneliness in our own ways. With the loss of his wife, home, business, and his two older children who'd moved out of state, and left with the responsibility of raising us, Dad turned to drinking.

My little sister stopped talking to either of us, which left me to continue my crying routine every night, buckled over in pain by a stomach ulcer. I'm not sure our pain would have eased any if we'd moved far away, but we lived only fifteen minutes from Mom. I would understand her not wanting to see us if she lived farther away, but she was close enough for me to see her in town. On occasions when I did see her laughing and smiling with her friends, she turned away from me. Her actions confirmed what I already knew to be true—we no longer existed. Her life consisted of having a good time, while ours barely hung on by a thread as we continued each day without her. But that was about to change for me.

When I turned sixteen, my mom reached out. I answered the phone when it rang.

"Amy? It's your mother."

I knew who she was, but after two years of not hearing her voice, I guess she felt the need to remind me.

"I've missed you and want you to come live with me," she said.

My heart did somersaults. I wanted to be angry with her but couldn't. I missed my mom and needed her, but I also dreaded telling Dad of my decision to go. His reaction didn't surprise me. First anger, then silence. I struggled with the feeling I'd betrayed him. Once my siblings found out, they screamed and cursed at me before also giving me the silent treatment. My family had mastered the art of silence and isolation. I never wanted to hurt my dad or my brother and sisters, but I desperately wanted Mom to want me again. I needed her to love me.

I would soon learn the hard way that moving in with Mom was a bad idea, but my decision may have been influenced by my then boyfriend, Greg. When Dad moved us into the house across town after the rest of the family moved out, Greg became physically abusive. He didn't like me going to a new school and constantly screamed and accused me of talking to other guys. After school I worked at a fast-food restaurant. Greg sat inside and watched me to see if I was talking to any guys. Once, at the end of my shift when I rounded the counter to mop the floor, he confronted me and accused me of smiling at a customer when I had taken his order. In Greg's fury, he slapped me. It wasn't the first time he'd hit me, but it was the first time in front of others. The police were called.

"Go home, Amy," my manager said. "He's banned from coming here again."

Devastated and embarrassed, I sat in my car in the parking lot and cried. When I arrived home, my little sister met me.

"Greg's been here." She glanced in the direction of my room. I approached and stood in the doorway of my destroyed bedroom. My belongings were strewn everywhere along with shattered pictures. Dad tried to clean up the broken glass. He looked around the room, then at me.

"This is your fault. If he ever shows up here again, I'm calling the police!"

I turned my cheek away from him, hoping he wouldn't see the redness from where Greg had slapped me. I didn't tell Dad what had happened at work. I didn't want him to be any more disappointed in me than he already was.

Greg continued to harass and threaten me, and he also made threats to my friends. I told them it was okay if they didn't want to be around me anymore because I didn't want anyone getting hurt. Deep down it wasn't okay, and it broke my heart. I kept reminding myself I was better off being alone. So why did I make the decision to reconnect with Mom? From the moment I walked into her apartment with my bag of clothes I sensed I'd made a mistake.

Mom's new life without her kids consisted of parties every night with people coming in and out at all hours drinking and getting high, including my mom. She fell down drunk daily. Unprepared for her new lifestyle, I tried to avoid her. If I wasn't at school or work, I stayed in my bedroom. We were strangers, and I realized at this point that there had always been a distance between us. I didn't know how to talk to her, so after the first couple of weeks, I wrote a letter telling Mom how much it hurt me to see her drunk night after night. My mom and her boyfriend were sitting on the couch when I walked into the living room and handed her the letter.

"What's this?" she asked.

"I wanted to share some things with you."

She read the letter, looked at me, and laughed. Then she balled the letter up and threw it across the room. If she didn't care about me then why had she asked me to move in with her? Had anything really changed between us? I kept my mouth shut and, after a few minutes of awkward silence, I went to my room and cried.

Why did I hold on to the illusion I could move back in with my mom and everything would be all better? I blamed only myself for the lies I believed, but I stayed even after the night a gun was pointed at my head.

Someone screamed from the other room. I left my bedroom to check on Mom. I walked down the hall, turned the corner to go into the living room, and stopped with a shotgun pointed at my head. Two of the drunken guys had argued, and one went outside and came back with a gun. As he aimed it at the other guy I stepped into the line of fire. A couple of the women screamed. The man with the gun looked from me to the other guy then back at me. He pointed the gun downward, turned, and left.

I remained frozen to the floor. When I could move, I ran back to my room and lay on the bed, my emotions running wild. One of Mom's friends checked on me.

"You okay, honey?" Her bloodshot eyes showed concern.

I pulled away when she reached to touch my hair. "I'm fine."

"You sure?"

"Yes," I lied. I wished it were true, but I hadn't been fine for a long time.

My mom's party continued as if nothing had happened. I waited for her to come see if I was all right, but she continued to party with no regard to the emotional trauma I'd faced. I wished he had pulled the trigger.

On another night I heard screaming again. This time it sounded like my mom. I rushed into the living room where a drunk couple were fighting.

"Get out," Mom yelled at both.

"Oh yeah? I think *you* need to leave." He grabbed my mom by her arm and shoved her out the front door. She stumbled down the concrete steps then cried out in pain.

I screamed, "Leave my mom alone!"

He turned, grabbed me by the arm, and shoved me through the open sliding-glass doors. I rolled down the hill into the parking lot. When he left, I headed back to the apartment. Mom had broken her elbow. One of her friends took her to the hospital while one of mine took me to the police station to file charges against the man.

"Sorry, you're too young." The policeman barely acknowledged me and my friend as we stood there. "You need a parent to sign the paperwork."

Disbelieving, I headed home and waited for my mom. Her anger was almost palpable when I explained what I'd tried to do.

"You did what? Stay out of my business. You had no right to go to the police. I'm not signing papers."

"He threw us out of our apartment," I said.

"My place, my friends." She headed to her room and slammed the door.

My concern for our safety was more important than her friends. Her friends were more important to her than my safety. In her eyes, *I* caused trouble, not her friends.

A week or so later I returned home from work to find several people passed out, or so I thought, on the living room floor. Exhausted, I headed to bed and fell asleep, only to be awakened by one of the guys from the other room in my bed with his hand inside my underwear. Fear and panic rushed over me. No, not again!

"I'll scream for my mom." I pushed against him.

He laughed. "Go ahead. She won't do anything about it."

Knowing he was right hurt as badly as what he was doing to me. I screamed for my mom's boyfriend. People knew he was crazy and always carried a gun. My assailant jerked his hand away and quickly left my room. I jumped up and locked my bedroom door. I climbed back into bed, curled into a tight ball, and cried myself to sleep. From then on, I kept my bedroom door locked. I told my mom what had happened, and she laughed at me for being so upset. People could continue to abuse me, and there was no one there to protect me. Why had I said anything? I shut down. My only safe place was inside myself where I hid from everybody and everything.

Sometime after that incident, I found myself collapsed on the kitchen floor where my heart felt like it would explode and at the same time my chest felt constricted with a crushing weight. Unable to catch my breath, I started to hyperventilate. Mom's friend Beth found me on the floor. She took me straight to my family doctor, and he informed me I'd suffered from another anxiety attack. This was the worst one I'd ever experienced.

"Amy, I'm concerned you're having a nervous breakdown. I'd like to give you a prescription for Xanax. It should help. Make an appointment to see me again in two weeks." He left the examination room.

After taking the medicine for two days, I discovered Mom had searched my room and stolen the rest of the pills. I couldn't tell the doctor I needed more. With my history of suicide attempts he probably would have believed I'd swallowed all the medicine. And if by some miracle he did believe me, I could get my mom in trouble. I never went back, and I kept my mouth shut. My life continued to spiral out of control. I missed a lot of school. When I overslept, I'd asked Mom why she hadn't woke me.

Almost every time she shrugged. "I didn't know you had school today."

I chose not to go if it meant being late. There really wasn't a reason to go since I couldn't focus or comprehend what the teachers taught anyway. When I did go, I sat in class and tried to listen. The teacher's mouth moved, and I heard her words but immediately afterward had no idea what was said. Frustrated, I felt like I'd lost my mind. I was alive but not living. I didn't want to live. I didn't want to feel.

What is wrong with me? I can't do anything right.

After I'd moved in with Mom, I met with Dad on Friday afternoons, and he'd give me money to buy food for the following week. I'd go straight to the grocery store to buy what I needed, then would hide the food in my bedroom closet. I only took out what I needed to fix a meal. If I didn't keep my food safe, my mom or her friends would eat everything and leave me with nothing.

After two months of this, Mom decided I needed to give her my money from Dad.

"It's costing me to have you living here. You need to carry your weight with the expenses," she said.

"I can't give it to you, Mom," I replied.

How did I cost her money when I bought my own food and paid for my own gas to go back and forth to work and school? As far as living there, I stayed away as much as possible and, when I was in the apartment, remained in my bedroom.

"If I give it to you, how will I be able to buy the things I need?"

"I want you to get out of my house." She glared at me.

The illusion of my mother loving and wanting me ended with harsh reality. My mom didn't want me, she wanted the money Dad gave me to live on. What a fool I'd been to think I could make her love and want me. I asked myself over and over, *why do people I love hurt me?* I thought of many reasons why, and all of them were my fault. I packed my clothes while Mom partied in the living room with her friends. I couldn't bear to look at her. I called a friend to pick me up and take me back to my dad's. When she agreed, I threw my bag of clothes out the bedroom window and climbed out. Sitting on the curb, I cried until she arrived. A couple of days after I moved out, I called my mom. She wouldn't talk to me. Instead, her boyfriend did.

"Once you're out, you're always out," he said.

I heard Mom telling him what to say.

"Hang up the phone," she said somewhere behind him. The call ended.

My lack of a relationship with my mom hurt but no longer surprised me. I grew increasingly numb to her actions and words. After having my own children, I couldn't imagine my life without them. How could Mom have continued to turn her back on us?

Dad never asked what happened to make me leave Mom's place, and I never offered to tell him. I figured my time there was my punishment for leaving him, and I deserved everything that happened. When would it all be over?

CHAPTER 7

Unforgettable Choices

After I moved back in with my dad, I grew more and more depressed. Having already struggled for three years with sadness and loneliness, I convinced myself I deserved every ounce of pain I experienced. All the bad things in my life had to be my fault. I'd reached a point of no longer caring what happened to me and lost all hope of ever finding happiness, because I wasn't worthy of anything good. I had no desire to see tomorrow, let alone imagine a future. With no love, security, or hope, I thought I had nothing else to lose.

Then I met Roger.

Roger came to the restaurant where I worked every morning to get breakfast. Sometimes he would stop by to say hi. I didn't believe him when he told me he was in jail serving time for malicious wounding but was on work release during the day. He asked for my number, and when he called the same night, I had to accept the collect call from the jail. Most people would call that a red flag, right?

During the next two weeks we talked several times a day. He continued to come by in the mornings, stop by after work, and call me every night. I didn't judge him for being incarcerated. I thought he was a good person. I used to think I was a good person, but I had caused so much pain to my family and others. Who was I to judge?

I warned Roger about my ex-boyfriend, Greg, who still stalked me and threatened anyone who paid attention to me, but he assured me he could take care of any situation. Would he be the one person willing to protect me? When Roger was released, he wanted to take me out. When he pulled into our driveway in a small pickup truck, I walked outside to meet him. I noticed someone else in the truck, then I realized I hadn't mentioned my date to anyone. And my dad and little sister weren't at home now to tell.

"Hi, Amy. Get in," Roger said.

The man sitting beside him stared ahead, not acknowledging my presence.

I walked to the passenger door, and Roger's friend got out to let me in. He stood about six feet three or taller and was very broad. He towered over my five six frame. At the time I weighed maybe one hundred pounds soaking wet.

"Hi," I said, but he still refused to look at me. I immediately felt sick but slid into the middle. He got in and shut the door. We pulled out of the driveway. "Where are we going?" I asked.

"To hang out with friends," Roger said.

He took back roads, and as it grew darker, I had no clue where we were. The farther we drove, the tighter the knot in my stomach grew. I felt tension growing between Roger and his companion, who I called the giant since he hadn't told me his name. He continued to avoid looking at me. Did he know something I didn't? And with his release from jail, why wasn't Roger happy? The smiling, talkative man I'd known during the past couple of weeks seemed unhappy now. We drove for more than an hour in an awkward silence that eventually became deafening.

Finally, Roger turned off the gravel road and onto a driveway leading back into the woods. By then we drove in complete darkness. He turned the truck lights off as soon as a house came into view. When Roger turned off the engine, he grabbed my hand and pulled me toward the house. Everything about the ride was odd, and now a little voice inside my head screamed run! Why didn't I listen?

Once inside, I recognized a classmate from my old school.

"Hi." She approached me. "So, you've met my older brother."

I sighed with relief. Finally, someone spoke to me. We played a game of pool, and as soon as the game ended Roger grabbed my hand again. "Come on." He led me into a room at the back of the house. When he turned on the light, we were standing in a bedroom. He shut and locked the door. My heart raced, and my stomach knotted in my throat.

He pulled me close and whispered in my ear, "You know what I want."

"No." I tried to push him away.

He grabbed my arms and squeezed. "Don't fight me." Roger pushed me onto the bed.

The more I pleaded for him to stop, the more aggressive he became. He pinned me down with his forearm and unzipped my pants with his other hand. I squirmed, trying to push him off, and continued to beg him to stop.

"Shut up." He slapped me. After removing my pants, he removed his own.

In a state of panic, I felt my heart beating in my ears. I struggled to swallow. There was nothing I could do; he was too strong.

I cried and tried to push him off again. I felt like his sister and the giant had to have heard us. So many disturbing thoughts raced through my mind. Why didn't they try to stop him? Had his friend refused to look at me earlier because he knew of Roger's plan? Would he hurt me next? If I found a way to escape from Roger, where would I go? I had no idea where I was or how far it was to another house. Were they going to kill me? How would anyone find me, when no one knew where I'd gone or who I was with? Would they go free if they murdered me?

I stared at the ceiling and cried. My mind and body went numb, and I no longer felt like I was a part of my own body. I no longer felt the weight of his body, heard the sounds he made, or smelled his revolting stench.

The assault continued until the giant banged on the door. "Somebody's coming."

Roger jumped off me and grabbed my clothes. He threw them at me and screamed, "Get them on now!"

We dressed quickly then he pulled me out of the room where his friend waited. Dragging me behind him, we ran out a back door and headed toward the truck. Roger shoved me inside, and all three of us left. He turned the headlights on when the house was out of sight. As we drove in silence again questions raced through my mind. What would they do to me now? Where was Roger's sister? I didn't see or hear her when we ran out. Did she leave? Was she unable to face me because of what her brother had done? Did the man sitting beside me hurt her? Why did we leave so fast? How could I have been so stupid? I continued to make all the wrong choices—choices ending with me being violated by men. Again, it was my fault and my punishment for going on a date with Roger, an ex-convict. Why was I so messed up?

After we drove for an hour, I recognized landmarks and knew we were headed in the direction of my dad's house. Was he taking me home? To my surprise and relief, Roger soon pulled into Dad's driveway. The porch light was on, and my car was the only one there. I rushed from the truck into the house and locked the door. Grabbing my dad's loaded pistol, I sat at the top of the stairs and listened for the sounds of someone trying to get in. My heart raced and hands shook as I pointed the gun toward the bottom of the stairs. We never locked any doors or windows at my dad's house, which meant there were many ways to enter, but there was only one way to get upstairs. My best chance to stop an intruder was on the stairs where I waited, prepared to shoot to kill. I had no intention of allowing Roger to kill me in my own home. That wouldn't make any sense if he tried, but then again what in my life over the past three years had made any sense?

After sitting there for nearly ten minutes, I crawled to the window facing the driveway and peeked out. Roger's truck was nowhere in sight. I went to every room in the house and locked the windows, never letting go of the gun. Thank God. Could this nightmare really be over? After securing the house, I grabbed clean clothes from my bedroom, ran downstairs to the bathroom, and locked the door. I turned the shower on as hot as I could stand and scrubbed until my skin felt raw and the water turned cold. Roger's smell still clung to me. I screamed then broke down and cried. I managed to pull myself back together enough to dry off and get dressed. The silence in the house confirmed nobody was home. I was too emotionally drained to pretend I was okay. The thought of facing my dad or sister made me physically ill. But being home alone scared me more. I unlocked the front door to allow my family to get in when they returned home, then went to bed and wept with Dad's gun under my pillow.

The next morning, I refused to tell my dad or little sister how I'd screwed up again. I couldn't handle someone else reminding me it was my fault; I placed enough guilt and shame on myself. At sixteen, my mind, body, and soul were exhausted. No wonder

I struggled with my faith. The events of the previous three years weighed heavily on me and ate away at my belief in a loving and protecting God.

But through all my anger I never stopped praying. I am not sure why. My daily prayers weren't always pleasant because most of the time I ranted. Who else but God did I have to take my anger and pain out on? But I wanted to believe everything I had been taught growing up in church. I never stopped believing in Him, but I couldn't understand how He allowed these things to happen to me, one of His children. Was I being punished by Him? Abandoned? I wondered if maybe my grandmother was right, and I had the devil in me. Maybe that's why God had turned His back and allowed my suffering. Maybe He believed me to be a bad seed.

It has taken many years to realize I was not alone the night Roger raped me. The scars were deep and damaging, but I was not alone.

After my experience with Roger, I reunited with Greg. He hurt and scared me, but he said he loved me. I wanted so desperately for someone to love me. Yes, I would rather be loved part of the time than have no love at all, even if I couldn't feel it or believe him. Everywhere I turned someone hurt me, so why even try to protect myself?

I could no longer handle the constant harassment and fear. I never knew where Greg was hiding, and I didn't have the strength to fight him. It would be better and safer for me to keep my enemy close. Eventually, I told Greg about what had happened with Roger.

"I told him no, and he forced me to have sex with him." I couldn't bring myself to say the word *raped*.

I don't think Greg believed me. Over the next seven years, he constantly brought it up and forced me to relive that night so many times, I doubted the truth. I hated him as much as I hated

Roger for sexually assaulting me. Ten years later I admitted the truth to myself. I didn't deserve what Roger had done to me, and I certainly didn't ask for it. But I had made an unforgettable choice and carried the guilt and shame for something done to me. Sometimes I wondered if, when I'd left my body the night I was raped, I had ever really come back. To this day, I believe a part of me never did.

I finished tenth grade and didn't go back. Not because I hated school but because Greg's constant accusations of me doing something or talking to somebody wore me down. Why go if I continued to be so stressed, and I couldn't comprehend what the teachers taught? I continued to work, but it took every ounce of energy and strength to get through my shifts. I lived in a fog, broken and defeated.

Twenty-four years after my horrible night with Roger, he returned to prison for first-degree murder, breaking and entering, kidnapping, arson, burglary with the intent to commit arson while armed with a deadly weapon, use of a firearm in the commission of a felony, and possessing a firearm after being convicted as a violent felon.

If I'd spoken up and pressed charges, could I have prevented the other victims in his path from the terror he caused and the life he took? Maybe, just maybe? But also maybe I couldn't have.

CHAPTER 8

Roles Reversed

Your mom's in her bathroom with a loaded gun. She's threatening to kill herself!" Mom's friend Beth found me in the middle of my shift at a fast-food restaurant and dropped this bombshell. With tears in her eyes, she spoke in a shaky voice. "She wants to talk to you."

I went to my manager, said I had a family emergency, grabbed my stuff, and ran out with Beth. My mom's apartment was only a couple miles from my work, and we arrived in a matter of minutes. Mom had been incapable of comforting me when I needed her the most, and now the roles were reversed. I had a choice to make. Walk out on her the same way she did to me or be the person I'd wished she could have been. Pretending not to care meant I wasn't any better than my mom. That wasn't me or the person I wanted to be.

I didn't know what to expect when we arrived at her apartment. Would Mom be on the floor with a gunshot wound? Was she waiting to kill herself in front of me because this was somehow my fault? These questions ran through my mind as we pulled into the apartment parking lot. I hesitated for a moment before running into the apartment calling her name. I stood outside the bathroom and begged her to unlock the door. Heartbroken and afraid, I listened to Mom's sobs. I continued to talk to her as I sat on the hallway floor. After what seemed an eternity, she opened the door. Seeing her red and swollen eyes, I wanted to hug her and take her pain away, but I didn't. Since she never showed affection, I didn't want to make the situation more awkward. I followed her to the kitchen where we sat at the table.

Mom sniffed. "I know all four of you kids hate me. Maybe I shouldn't have left your dad."

She seemed to wait for my response, but I didn't know how to answer her. She'd caused a lot of pain, not only because she'd left my dad, but because she'd left all of us and chosen not to be involved in our lives. Yet I knew telling the truth would make the situation worse. Instead, I told her what she wanted to hear to ease her pain. After we talked and she calmed down, Mom removed the diamond ring my dad had given her and handed it to me.

"I want you to have it. You're the only one who cares for me."

I accepted the ring and wondered if she had finally decided to be the mom my older siblings told me she'd been to them. One who would love and protect my little sister and me and offer us a life that included her. Afraid to leave my mom alone, I stayed the night. I tossed and turned all night long, concerned she might get up and try to hurt herself. The next morning, she acted as if nothing happened. Stunned and confused, I didn't know what to say. After having her coffee, she asked for the ring back, and later in the day she went back to partying with her friends. Mom never acknowledged her crisis ever happened.

Because of her I'd lost my job when I left in the middle of my shift. (I hadn't waited on my manager's reply. I just ran out.) When I told Mom, she replied, "That's your problem, not mine." At that point, I don't know why I didn't go back to Dad's house, but I continued to stay at my mom's. Or it is better to say that I *attempted* to stay there.

I did find another job working at a local restaurant on the third shift—eleven at night to seven in the morning. I washed dishes, bused tables, and helped get the restaurant ready for the breakfast crowd. One morning, not long after starting my new job, Mom didn't pick me up from work. I needed to get ahold of her because I didn't have a key to the apartment. When I couldn't reach her, another waitress allowed me to sleep at her house. At first, I called my mom every day, but she never answered her phone. Two weeks later, she contacted me at work to let me know she'd be there after my shift. We got into a big fight at the apartment that day. I was angry she'd forgotten me, and she was angry I'd had the nerve to say anything about it. I was done. I grabbed my things and headed back to my dad's.

Looking back, I realize I was the only one weak enough to continue the roller-coaster ride of attempting to have a relationship with her. Mom used me and my emotions as if they were part of a game. One she was winning. I didn't want to play her game anymore; I wanted a parent who would protect me. Mom and I didn't speak again for more than a year.

CHAPTER 9

Beaten and Broken

My daughter, Cynthia, was born on February 3, 1990, exactly thirty days after I turned eighteen.

At the time, I lived with my dad, little sister, and controlling boyfriend, Greg, who had stayed with my family on and off since I was fourteen. Even after the incident when he flew into a rage, destroyed my room, and my dad had threatened to call the police, Dad allowed Greg back into our home.

My little sister called Mom and told her about Cindy's birth. Mom called a couple days after we returned home from the hospital and, after more than a year of me not seeing her, asked to see her granddaughter.

"If you want to see my daughter, you know where we live," I told her. Harsh words maybe, but I was tired of being the only one to make an effort at a relationship. I had nothing left in me to try.

Mom came over a couple of times. We never discussed what had happened between us, which was okay with me. No words could have changed what took place, so there was no point in bringing it up.

After becoming a mother, I really missed our family being together. My sister Lisa had given birth to a daughter seven months prior to me having Cindy. She had moved back home to be with us for a short time when she was pregnant but eventually returned to Virginia Beach. Brian also moved from Delaware to Virginia Beach. Even though my siblings lived a four-hour drive from us, we only visited once. Brian happened to be visiting the day I went into labor. I was happy he met my baby girl.

Seven months after the birth of our daughter, Greg and I married and moved into our own place. Everyone seemed happy we were married, but I had done so out of fear, afraid he would hurt Cindy or me if I didn't.

After a particularly bad incident, Greg apologized to me. People who heard the apology believed him and, in the end, defended him. No matter how badly Greg hurt me, his friends and family members told me I needed to give him another chance because he was sorry. He cried to his family one minute and, as soon as we were alone, made me feel like he could kill me and get away with it the next. As messed up as it sounds, I felt safer for my daughter and me to be with him than live in fear of the price I would pay if I left.

Because my dad expected me to marry Greg after the birth of our child, I never told him about the abuse. I didn't want to disappoint him like I'd done so many times in the past. He never knew of the occasions I'd called Greg's sister to come get us because I feared for our safety.

In truth, I wasn't safe no matter where I lived. I didn't know what it felt like to feel safe, yet I desperately wanted to know. I went back to Greg every time because I had nowhere else to go. We both knew his promise of no more abuse was a lie. I was trapped, and we both knew it. I couldn't return home and tell my dad about anything. He would be devastated. Knowing there was not a single person in my life who could keep me safe, I applied what I'd already learned—I kept my mouth shut and suffered in silence or else wish I'd had.

Greg did everything he could to keep me captive. He claimed he put something across the bottom of the driveway so he'd know if I left the house. Only he knew the location of the device. I didn't believe him, but questioning him really wasn't worth another argument. He made sure I didn't have friends so there was nowhere for me to go. Once he hid a voice-activated tape recorder near the telephone to see if I called anyone while he was at work. The phone was also close to the washing machine and dryer. On a day I did laundry, Greg returned home furious because all he heard on the recorder were the sounds from the washing machine and dryer. He swore I had done it on purpose. As the mental abuse grew, so did the physical abuse.

A year into our marriage, during another big fight, I fell to the floor and thought Greg was going to kill me.

"Mommy!" Cindy screamed in my ear while sitting on the floor next to me.

At almost two, she'd witnessed too much abuse in her short life.

Unable to speak or take a breath, spots appeared in my eyes. Was this it? Would I finally die? My body grew weak. I didn't want to fight any longer. Before I lost consciousness I thought about Cindy. Was I leaving my daughter in the hands of a monster to face the same abuse I had? Out of nowhere, I gained enough energy to shove him off. My throat burned as I coughed. Grabbing Cindy, I tried to get away.

My husband cried out, "Please don't go, Amy. I'm sorry." His sobs shook his body. "It won't happen again. I promise." He looked from me to Cindy, then back to me. "Please."

Again another lie. Again I stayed. I couldn't look at or talk to him. I hated him. But I hated myself for what my daughter witnessed on a regular basis. I carried our daughter to the bedroom. She gently wrapped her arms around my neck, so different from what my husband had done to me. I sat on the bed and rocked her in my arms, trying to soothe her as much as trying to soothe myself. How could I get us out of this?

The abuse continued into my second pregnancy. A fall caused me to bleed and cramp. I went to the doctor the next morning.

After examining me, the doctor said, "There's nothing that can be done until you're further along in your pregnancy."

I prayed nonstop for God to let me keep my baby. I continued to have contractions, and as soon as I reached my fifth month my doctors put me on medication to prevent me from going into premature labor. As my contractions increased so did the amount of medicine I received.

"You must stay in bed until it's time to deliver," one doctor ordered me.

I left the appointment shaking my head. With an active two-year-old and no one to help me, the doctor's request was impossible. I hated my husband—the father of the child I carried—for putting our unborn baby's life in jeopardy. My third trimester brought more stress.

"Your baby may not survive." The somberness in the doctor's eyes caused my fear to increase. "You have a tear in your uterus. If the baby gets any bigger, he could possibly get stuck in the tear and strangle himself."

My hands shook as I placed them on my abdomen and tried to take in the information. I continued to pray. *God, please let me keep my baby*. He answered my prayer. At twenty, I gave birth a second time. Dustin was born July 1, 1992. I called him my miracle baby.

With no job, no money, and no family or friends to run to, I decided it was time to make a change. One I wound up fighting every step of the way.

CHAPTER 10

Loss

Two months after Dustin's birth I decided to go back to school. Never finishing high school had weighed on my heart, but I knew Greg would not be happy about my decision. I didn't care. I signed up for the next available GED class before I told him.

"You're not going." He raised his voice, ready to fight.

"I've already signed up for the next available GED class."

"You did this without talking to me? I don't like it." Greg balled his fists by his sides.

"I'm going back to school." I turned and walked out of the room before things escalated.

I wasn't surprised he was angry and against the idea since he was one of the reasons I hadn't finished high school. I hadn't fought for my diploma the first time, but I would fight the second go round. I hadn't been a student since sixteen and—at the age of twenty, with a two-year-old, a six-month-old, and an abusive husband—the cards seemed stacked against me, but I was determined.

During my first GED class, and for the first time since I'd been married, I made a friend.

"Hi," a classmate said that first class.

My mind still on the fight I'd had with Greg, I glanced around to see if she'd meant to speak to me. I'd sat alone during my first

GED class and was surprised when someone approached me afterward.

"I'm Debbie," she said.

We discovered we only lived a mile away from each other, and our children were close in age. We exchanged phone numbers. Her friendship would become my saving grace. For the first time in my life, I had a shoulder to cry on.

Debbie encouraged me to dig deeper and keep moving regardless of the circumstances. Thirty years later, we're still the best of friends and love each other unconditionally. Years after we first met, Debbie said she approached me because I had sat in class alone with a black eye. She believed she needed to talk to me. I don't remember the black eye, but I'm so glad she wanted to speak to me.

I met Debbie's husband, Jeff, a few days after when I went to their house to study for our big math test. Our children played together. When Debbie and I were stuck on an algebra section, Jeff entered the kitchen to try and teach us. I admired him for trying to help us and how supportive and proud he was of Debbie.

"You're having an affair with her aren't you," Greg confronted me after I returned one evening from studying at Debbie's.

I ignored him. His accusatory words along with his rants and threats had decreased in their effects on me. He had succeeded in isolating me for four years, but no more. Two months later I proudly walked across the stage and received my GED. After getting my diploma, I enrolled in Central Virginia Community College, again against the will of my husband and without his support. I qualified for a Pell Grant, which paid for my tuition, books, and supplies. Determined to continue turning my life around, I entered the Early Childhood Education Program, totally scared to death.

I made the Dean's list for the two semesters I completed, both times with straight A's. With the constant fights, screaming matches, accusations, and threats for going to class or doing homework, Greg made going to school a nightmare and made it nearly impossible for me to study. For the life of me I don't know how I made straight A's those first two semesters. But once again Greg's behavior soon forced me to drop out of the program.

My husband knew school was important to me but my children more so. They were all I had. I couldn't imagine living without them, yet I'm grieved at not being able to remember their infant or toddler years. In all honesty, I have very few memories of my teenage years through my early thirties. The memories I do have, I wished I didn't. The journals I kept beginning at age thirteen tell me of the life I experienced during those missing years. They've allowed me to share my story. It's a shame that to block out the painful memories, the good memories are also taken away. My marriage along with the emotional scars from my adolescence took a toll on my health. I had trouble breathing, constant headaches, back and chest pains, and a stomach ulcer that I'd dealt with since the age of fourteen. I went to see a doctor when I had a hard time swallowing.

The doctor checked my chart. "You're dealing with anxiety. That's why you're suffering from chest and back pains. Your throat is swelling from stress, which is making it difficult to swallow. If you don't correct the root of the problem, Amy, you're going to die." She held my gaze until I looked away and fought back tears. She handed me several prescriptions, including muscle relaxers.

"Remember what I said."

I nodded before she walked out of the room. Finally allowing the tears to run down my face, I looked at my children playing on the floor. *I can't leave them.*

After I got the kids buckled into their car seats, I opened one of the prescription papers the doctor had handed me. On it was the phone number of an abused woman's shelter, as well as the phone number for a lawyer. I broke down and cried again.

My daughter said, "Mommy, why are you crying?"

"Mommy just doesn't feel good," I said.

Even though I had never told anyone my husband was abusive, they knew, which caused me to feel embarrassed and weak. I hid the phone numbers so Greg wouldn't find them. The abuse would have worsened if he thought I'd told someone he hurt me, but I couldn't bring myself to throw the information away. Deep down, I knew I might need it some day.

Our destructive relationship affected not only my health but also how my children acted. Three-year-old Dustin refused to have anything to do with his dad. He screamed and cried if Greg came near me. Most mornings I woke to find Dustin sleeping on the floor beside my bed or sleeping under my bed with only his little feet sticking out. Afraid his dad would hurt me, he didn't want to leave my side.

Cindy had a different approach. When her dad came home from work and yelled, she'd tell him to go back to work. Greg swore I had told her to say it. But she said the things I wished I'd said but never did. I no longer could walk into another room or outside without her following me and asking, "Mommy, are you crying?"

One day Cindy and I were sitting outside on the porch steps when Greg came out and yelled about something, then went back into the trailer.

She turned to me.

"Mommy, I don't want to live here anymore."

The brutal honesty of my five-year-old was exactly what I needed to wake up from the fog I was living in and realize the time had come to get my children out. Unfortunately, I didn't leave soon enough.

I stopped sleeping in the same room and slept in the living room thinking I would feel safer on the couch, but I didn't. I'd lie there with my eyes closed for hours, night after night, and listen for the sound of Greg getting a knife so I could brace myself for what would come next. Night after night I waited and wondered if it was going to be the night I died. In time I welcomed the thought of him killing me. It would be a blessing to have my nightmare over. I believed dying by his hands would be better than continuing to live in constant fear.

I left Greg when I was twenty-three, after having endured nine years of his abuse. My daughter was five, and my son was three. My children deserved better. I'd saved and hidden enough babysitting money to put a deposit and first month's rent on an apartment in a nearby town. The people I babysat for told me they would continue to bring their kids to me after I moved. I wanted a normal life for the children and me, but Greg made sure we felt his wrath for the next year and five months.

My estranged husband attempted everything in his power to get me to return out of fear. He followed me day or night, regardless of the time. I received threating phone calls at all hours of the night and on a continual basis. I couldn't eat or sleep. I was exhausted, and my nerves were shot. I dropped down to ninety-nine pounds and looked like death. I refused to give in to him but constantly looked over my shoulder while trying to pick up the pieces of our broken life and making a new home. When Greg realized I was not returning, he changed his tactic.

After arriving home from work one day, I listened to a disturbing answering machine message from him. I felt my children's lives were in danger. I stared at the machine as chills ran down my spine and my heart beat faster. I grabbed my children and the tape from inside the answering machine and drove straight to the police department to file a protective order against Greg. An emergency hearing was set for the next day because the kids were scheduled to go to his house the same day.

Where we lived you could not tape record someone without their knowledge and use it in court. However, the taped message on the answering machine from Greg was allowed because he knew the threatening message was being recorded. After nine years of abuse and doing and saying anything he wanted to me, his crying and attempts to make himself look like a victim didn't work. Finally, he was going to be held accountable. The judge granted the protective order and stopped Greg's visitations until he completed a series of anger management classes.

The judge asked me to stay behind and asked everyone else to leave the courtroom. When the door closed, he removed his glasses and looked at me for an awkward silence. Then he sighed.

"Ms. Kunkle, the protective order is just a piece of paper. If you stay in the county, there are only two deputies on duty at a time. If you called 911, it could take forty-five minutes before anyone would get to your house." He seemed to want me to respond.

"I understand," I managed to say.

"A lot of unlawful things can happen in forty-five minutes. The only way for you and the children to be safe would be to move to the city where the police can respond faster. Is there anyone there you can stay with?"

Not if I wanted my children to be safe. I shook my head. Mom was the only person I knew who lived in the city, and her house was not a place for kids, nor would she want us. Dad wasn't an option either since I hadn't talked to him in a long time. When we'd tried to visit, his girlfriend locked the door and pretended no one was home. Dad had called me when he found out I'd left Greg and screamed at me for splitting up my family. I had said nothing as he spewed accusations. When he was done with his tirade, he had hung up. I never told him about the abuse.

Over a period of seventeen months, I obtained several protective orders against Greg. His visitation with the children was suspended several times, but occasionally he had supervised visits.

I told my little sister, Puddy, everything. Someone needed to know if I turned up missing or dead, my husband would probably be responsible. I told her about Dad's phone call, and she went to talk to him and told him of the years of abuse. He was disappointed I had never told him.

After court, Puddy moved in with me for a month before leaving for the navy. I felt safer having her with us. Puddy and I only had each other, because neither of us had a relationship with other family members. Besides my children and my best friend, Debbie, she was all I had. When she left, I was crushed. With no hope of a normal, happy life, I suffered from extreme guilt and shame. I blamed myself for what I'd allowed my children to live through. Why hadn't I protected them better? Why wasn't I strong enough to stand up for them? Or for me? What had I done for life to be so hard and full of so much pain for twelve long years?

Little did I know, my suffering wasn't over, and many more tears were to come. But one thing I did know, after so many years of suffering, I had completely lost my faith in God.

CHAPTER 11

Second Chances

My divorce was final in November 1996. Greg continued to create drama by hurting me emotionally, and I continued to struggle with depression and cutting. Despite everything, I knew it was time to move on. Time for me to have a second chance at life, but was it even possible? Barely getting by with the money I made from babysitting during the day and working a part-time job at night, I decided to accept a full-time job working daytime hours on an assembly line. Affording a babysitter was beyond my means. After a lot of thought I called my mom and asked if she would be willing to watch Dustin until I could find someone else. He would be okay with her during the day since she only partied at night. My mom agreed.

When I was married, we only saw Mom on holidays and on rare visits. Since my separation, I visited a little more frequently. I still would leave her house feeling like I did as a teenager—never good enough. Yet a part of me still wanted and tried to have a real mother-daughter relationship.

Dustin made a new best friend while he stayed with my mom. He saw him every day when he went with my mom to pick up her boyfriend Charlie from work. There was another guy named Charlie, or as Dustin would call him "Lil Farley" because he couldn't say Charlie. This second Charlie worked with Mom's Charlie. Confused yet? It took a while for me to catch on that Dustin was not talking about my mom's Charlie. Dustin's new friend Lil Farley hung out at her house for a while after work, then she'd take him home in the evenings since he lived on the next street over. When I arrived at Mom's place to pick up Dustin, his new friend was always gone. Dustin loved Lil Farley. Maybe because he was an adult male who paid attention to him, and he seemed to fill Dustin's need for a father figure in his life.

Every day I heard something new about his friend until, finally, I decided I needed to find out who he was. I went to my mom's one Friday night when I didn't have the kids and I knew he was going to be there. Charlie (Lil Farley) was close to my age, and I thought he was attractive. Later in the evening, I got his phone number from mom's boyfriend, Charlie. He didn't want to give it to me because he thought he wouldn't be the right person for me. A couple nights later I called Charlie and asked him out on a date. He said yes.

Meanwhile my little sister, Puddy, now stationed in Louisiana, gave birth to her own daughter, Julia. Being a single mom and fourteen hours away from family, she decided she wanted to come home. She asked if I would take care of Julia until her discharge was finalized. Of course, I agreed. I would do anything for my little sister. A couple weeks after my niece was born, my sister Lisa went to Louisiana and brought them both back to my house. At the end of her six-week maternity leave, Puddy returned to Louisiana to arrange her navy discharge.

Taking care of three kids was a big adjustment physically and financially, but I made it work. Staying busy kept my mind occupied and distracted from my previous nightmares. My mom—already babysitting Dustin—agreed to watch Julia while I worked.

Greg had not paid any child support for more than a year, which caused money to be tight. There was no way I could afford a baby-sitter for two children.

With Cindy in kindergarten, my days consisted of dropping her off at school, driving thirty minutes to my mom's and dropping off the other two, then driving another thirty minutes to work. After work, I again had an hour and a half commute before we all returned home.

During all these changes with my family and household, Charlie came over for our first date. It was probably not the best timing, and I don't know if it would really be considered a date since we watched movies with Cindy, Dustin, Puddy, Julia, and Puddy's best friend, Dana. But I hadn't dated since I was fourteen, so what did I know?

At twenty-six, Charlie had never been married and didn't have kids. At twenty-six, I was divorced with a daughter soon to be seven, a four-year-old son, and a six-week-old niece. If Charlie was going to run, that was his opportunity.

My relationship with Charlie progressed quickly, almost too fast for both of us. A few short months after we began to date, I went to the doctor. I'd been bleeding for sixteen days and thought something was wrong. I never knew joy and sadness could be experienced so quickly in one statement.

"You're pregnant," the doctor told me. "But the bleeding means your body is trying to miscarry."

Five days later I lost the baby. I knew the exact minute our baby left my body. My heart sank, and I broke down as I stared at the remains of our child, one who would not have a chance at life. I wrapped the baby in toilet paper and screamed for Charlie. He walked into the bathroom, and I held out my hand. Even though

I was too early in my pregnancy for our child to resemble a baby, I knew.

"I lost the baby, *our* baby." I cried uncontrollably.

He stood there in silence.

"What should I do?" I couldn't flush or throw away the baby like trash. The thought made me cry harder.

"Do what you think is best." Charlie left the room.

After managing to pull myself together, I placed the carefully wrapped toilet paper into a resealable bag and buried it in the backyard. Even though I saw the pain on his face, Charlie refused to talk to me or acknowledge our loss. I had no other choice but to grieve alone.

My doctor estimated I had been between six to eight weeks along.

The pregnancy had not been planned. The timing was terrible. My ex-husband, Greg, constantly caused drama and took me to court over nothing. When I found out I was pregnant, Greg's harassment no longer mattered, nor did it distract me from the pain of my loss. So many years later my heart still aches at the loss of Charlie's and my first baby, and tears still fall freely. I look forward to the day I arrive in heaven and will be greeted by my sweet child.

After her navy discharge, Puddy moved in with me. She kept the kids during the day while I worked, and she left for work after I returned home. I found a job as a bookkeeper closer to my house, which saved me two hours of driving time, but I still struggled financially. I needed a second job and was offered a job as an exotic dancer to work on weekends for private parties in a nearby town. After talking it over with Charlie, I agreed to take the job even though I wasn't sure how I would pull it off. I had no self-esteem and couldn't stand for anyone to look at me. And I couldn't look anyone in the eyes. Because of my history, making eye contact signified defiance, a challenge. Also, I feared if anyone looked into my eyes, they would see all the pain I tried to hide. Lack of eye contact was a defense mechanism I needed to possess in the world of exotic dancing.

In the evenings, I left after the kids went to bed and arrived home long before they woke up. They never knew I was gone. Either Charlie or Puddy stayed with them while I worked. Drinking became a part of my work, and I drank enough to feel numb before my performances. Because I'd mastered the art of detachment years ago, I became a different person on stage. As easily as turning off a light switch, I shut out the world. Three months after starting my new job, I found out I was pregnant. Again, not planned. Charlie was extremely happy, and, after the shock wore off, I was too.

I thought by now my ex would see I'd moved on and so should he, but Greg's harassment continued. He would ride by my house late at night as if to see whether Charlie's truck were there, then make his presence known by spinning tires. Next thing I knew he wanted to take me to court for custody of my children because I lived immorally. The judge told me Charlie was not allowed to be at my house late at night. Either we needed to be married by the next court hearing or, if he found out Charlie still stayed with us, I would lose custody. I never imagined a judge would give custody to a father who lost his visitation rights multiple times and had been ordered to have supervised visits. But times were different back then.

I could not lose my children, but since I was pregnant with Charlie's child, it wouldn't have been fair to ask him to leave either.

And I loved him. I felt loved and safe for the first time in my life. Still, the thought of marrying again sent panic through me.

I was scared out of my mind and mentally not ready to enter another marriage. Yet Charlie and I made the decision together, and, before the next court date, we married on November 21, 1997, after only nine months of dating and three months into a pregnancy. I had never imagined Dustin's new best friend would become my husband and his stepfather.

We moved forty-five minutes away to start a new life. Everyone in my life at that time except for Puddy and Charlie, thought I had become a stay-at-home mom. But I continued to dance until I started to show at five months. Most of the time I worked for two hours and brought home double the money my husband did after he worked forty hours.

When Charles Thomas was born on June 4, 1998, Cindy was eight and Dustin was six. Cindy treated her little brother as though he were her baby. Even though Dustin loved Charles, he wasn't sure what to think of his new brother. He'd always been his momma's boy; he didn't want to share me.

I went back to dancing when Charles was eight weeks old. Over the next couple of years, I danced at private parties all over the state of Virginia and, for a short time, in a club in South Carolina. Living in a small town, word of my career eventually got out, and I quit when my dancing became harder to hide from Cindy and Dustin.

The first seven years of our marriage were extremely hard. There were days, sometimes weeks, when we didn't speak to each other. There were times I didn't know if we would make it because I was too broken for Charlie to understand me. He was quick tempered and had his own demons. On the occasions when he yelled, I had flashbacks of my violent past. The memories only lasted seconds, but the results lasted weeks. Stuck in protection mode, I'd pull inside myself to hide, determined not to make the same mistake by talking about how I felt. Charlie couldn't understand my continued struggle with depression and cutting. At first, he tried to get me to open up, but as I continued not to respond, he would stop asking. Every time I pulled myself out of the darkness, I knew there'd be a next time. And there was always a next time. But when my depression got the best of me, Charlie made sure we all got through it.

No matter what we faced in our marriage, I couldn't have asked for a better father for my children. I didn't always agree with Charlie's parenting, and I was protective of the kids, sometimes to a fault, but Charlie was a hero to the children. He loved Cindy and Dustin as though they were his own. For the longest time Dustin told everyone Charlie was his real dad. He told people they had the same blood. When Dustin wanted to play T-ball and they couldn't find a coach, Charlie took a class to become certified. He coached Dustin's team for two years. There was nothing he wouldn't do for his children.

Yet as much as I loved him, I was not able to let him love me. Maybe I was incapable of love. I didn't love me and believed God didn't either.

CHAPTER 12

The Price My Children Paid

Witnessing domestic violence can leave lasting effects that may not be immediately apparent. During my marriage to Greg, my two small children acted as my protectors, often worried and asking me if I was okay.

After I separated from Greg, five-year-old Cindy threw up every time her dad called or after she returned home from their visitations. After a series of tests, doctors discovered a small stomach ulcer. Her vomiting was stress related. I put her in therapy to give her a safe environment to talk about her feelings. I did not want my daughter to grow up with the same outlook as me—better to keep my mouth shut to survive.

At three, Dustin reacted with violent outbursts. In his anger he tried to strangle his sister multiple times. I knew Dustin mimicked what he witnessed in his environment, but I refused to allow the vicious cycle to continue and made up my mind to stop it. My ex-husband turned into his father, but my son would not turn into his.

After seven more years of abuse from Greg, Dustin hit rock bottom at the age of ten. As protective and guarded as I thought I wanted to be for my children, I found out it wasn't enough.

Cindy and Dustin both have very few memories of their childhood, and the memories they do have are ones they wished they didn't. The fact history had repeated itself caused me deep sadness. They had inherited the pain not of their own doing or choices but from my poor decision making and my brokenness.

The court had ordered Cindy and Dustin to spend every other weekend with their dad. We'd meet in a public place halfway between his house and mine. One Friday I pulled into the meeting spot with Cindy and Dustin sitting in the back seat. When Greg arrived and got out of his truck, Cindy opened the car door.

"Bye, Mom." She walked toward her dad.

Dustin jumped over the seat and climbed in between me and the steering wheel. He sat on my lap facing me, grabbed my shirt in both hands, and cried.

"Please don't make me go," he begged. The fear in his eyes as he looked at me with tears rolling down his face ripped my heart.

Completely lost for words, I said nothing. My son was ten and hadn't been on my lap since he was five years old. He continued to plead.

"Please, Mom, don't make me go, please."

By now Greg was at my car door. "Let's go, Dustin," he demanded.

"Okay, Dustin, you need to calm down," I said.

He continued to repeat in a whisper, "Please, Mom, please." He clutched my shirt with a death grip.

Greg screamed. "Get out of the car *now*."

Refusing to look at his father, Dustin continued to beg. The pure fear my son demonstrated told me something was very wrong.

"Can't you see he's upset? I'm not forcing him to get out of the car," I told a furious Greg.

"You listen to me, son. If you don't get out, I'll physically remove you myself." Greg's angry words caused Dustin to cry harder and grip me until I thought I would be crushed.

I refused to allow my son to go through any more pain. I pushed down the door lock button and rolled up the windows.

"It's okay. Everything is going to be okay. I won't make you go," I reassured Dustin.

As Greg walked toward his truck, he yelled over his shoulder, "I'm calling the police. I'll make sure you go to jail."

Dustin watched Greg get into his truck. His tears slowed, and his grip on my shirt lessened. Soon he climbed out of my lap and into the passenger seat and put on his seatbelt. He stared out the window as I pulled onto the highway, and we drove in silence. Halfway through the thirty-minute drive home I pulled into a church parking lot, turned off the car, and faced my son.

"What's wrong? Did something happen that I need to know about?"

He continued to stare out the window, never saying a word.

"I can only help you if you tell me what's going on."

I could see tears running down his face in the window's reflection, but he refused to look at me or respond. Completely helpless and confused, I started the car, and we continued toward home.

When we arrived, he went straight to his room, so I started dinner. I thought if I gave him some space, he would open up to me. He didn't. I tried again a couple hours later, but he refused to say a word or eat dinner. He stayed in his room the entire night.

I laid in bed trying to sleep. Desperate for answers, I remembered the kids' journals. Cindy was in fifth grade and Dustin in third when I pulled them out of school to be homeschooled. Mainly because Dustin's teacher asked for him to be tested for attention deficit disorder since he struggled with concentrating. After having him evaluated, the doctor put him on medication, but his teacher wanted his medication increased. After three increases in three months I said enough. Another reason for the homeschooling was because Dustin had been bullied because of his small size.

As part of their writing curriculum, they were required to write in a journal every day, anything they wanted. They knew this was the only schoolwork I wouldn't check so they could freely write and keep it private. I got out of bed that night and went into the room where we kept their schoolbooks. I picked up Dustin's journal and looked through it to see if I could gain any insight as to the cause of the evening's events. Nothing could have prepared me for what I found.

As I flipped through the pages, I didn't see anything concerning until the end of the entries. When I turned the final page, my heart sank. Dustin had drawn a graphic picture of him shooting and killing his father. There were only two words on the page— *me* over top of the picture of the person holding a gun, and *Greg* over the picture of the person lying in a pool of blood. There were several more pictures like the first one, all of them graphic, bloody, and of the same subject—Dustin killing his father. I found no explanation as to why he wanted his father dead. I sat there stunned. What would I do now?

Things were about to get worse. Soon after the visitation incident, I went to wake Dustin one morning. Blood stained his sheets. A lot of blood.

I flipped out. "Get out of bed, now. Strip down to your underwear."

He obeyed but didn't look at me. To cover all the wounds on his body took one and a half boxes of Band-Aids. When I took his sheets off the bed to wash them, a pair of tweezers fell to the floor.

He'd used tweezers to dig into his skin until he created ulcer-like wounds. I knew all too well how I had struggled with cutting, but my kids never knew I did or saw any wounds. Tears filled my eyes, and my stomach turned to knots. Why is my son doing this? What am I missing? The thought of my son hurting the same way I hurt devastated me.

"I'll stop, Mom," he promised without telling me why he had done it in the first place.

The next night, he used a tiny screwdriver to reopen some of the same wounds. Dustin grew angry and distant. He stayed by himself, lied about doing his schoolwork, and yelled at his sister and baby brother. One day I walked into the living room where Dustin had set a balled-up piece of paper on fire and put it in the middle of the floor. Was he attempting to burn down the house? Why was he spinning out of control? I didn't know how to help him.

With only a week until his next scheduled visit with his father, I knew I was running out of time to figure out the cause of his drastic change. Afraid I would wake up one morning and learn my son had taken his own life, I called around and found a psychiatric hospital to have him evaluated. I wasn't allowed to go with Dustin when he was escorted into a room for assessment. One hour later the therapist came out to talk to me.

"He doesn't need to be admitted, but I recommend outpatient therapy twice a week for depression and post-traumatic stress disorder," she said. "He's not sleeping. He told me he lies in bed awake at night because he believes his dad will try to hurt you. I suggest sleeping pills to help him get the sleep he needs."

Even though my ex and I had been divorced for seven years, Dustin continued to fear for my safety. The dark circles under his eyes weren't from his ADD medication but from staying awake at night.

My son had also told the counselor about the times his dad physically abused him.

What? With no time to process the counselor's words, she continued. "If he goes back to his dad's, Dustin will try to kill him. He openly shared about cutting himself, but most importantly, he's had suicidal thoughts."

How was I supposed to process these words? I sat there and allowed my tears to flow. I felt like a complete failure as a mother for not knowing. Was I so consumed by my own brokenness that I had totally missed my son's pain?

Once again, I was pulled back to the therapist's words. "I recommend you file papers to stop the visits with his father. Let's set up a weekly therapy session then reevaluate how he's doing," she said.

I went to the courthouse and filed the paperwork for an emergency hearing to temporarily stop visitation, only to find out Greg had been there after Dustin refused to go with him. He had filed charges against both of us for violating the court's visitation order. I could see him filing charges against me, but what kind of a monster files charges against his own ten-year-old son for refusing to allow him the opportunity to abuse him again? I was furious. I knew Greg's action was not about him wanting to see his son but all about having control.

An emergency hearing was set. The therapist wrote the judge a letter explaining the findings of Dustin's psychiatric evaluation and her recommendations for visitations to be suspended. In his chambers, the judge spoke to Dustin. I don't know what Dustin said, but the judge ordered the visitation between him and his father to be stopped immediately and also granted a fifteen day protective order.

After the hearing the judge told me, "There's no doubt in my mind if Dustin had been forced to go to his father's house, both of their pictures would be in the newspapers."

His statement sent a chill down my spine.

Regardless of the current judge's ruling, the case still needed to be placed on our regular judge's docket for him to evaluate the protective order, visitation rights, and the charges Greg had filed against us.

Dustin was appointed a guardian ad litem, an attorney to represent his best interest at the next hearing. Meanwhile, he continued with all his therapy sessions.

I hired an attorney because, if found guilty of the violation of a court order, I could face jail time. My attorney told me to make an appointment for another psychiatric evaluation from another therapist not in any way associated with the first. Even though he did not feel it would be imperative, it could only help Dustin. I had my child evaluated again and did not tell the therapist about his previous tests. The second therapist reached the same diagnosis and recommendations for counseling, medication, and no visitation with his father.

At the next hearing, I promised my son that everything would be okay and that Charlie and I would protect him. My attorney presented letters from both therapists stating my son had been abused by his father and suffered from depression and post-traumatic stress as a result. The judge granted the protective order and agreed that there was a finding of abuse by Dustin's father. He ordered Greg to lock up all the firearms to keep Dustin from using them against him. He ordered him not to put his hands on

Dustin and for Greg and Dustin to participate in family counseling together.

Dustin was to have visitation with his father for six hours every other Sunday, supervised by Cindy, his twelve-year-old sister, as recommended by Dustin's guardian ad litem. The guardian believed it was important for Greg and Dustin to maintain a relationship, even though the day before the hearing was the first time he'd ever spoken to Dustin and had never spoken to Dustin's therapist before making his recommendations.

As for the violation of the court order charges Greg filed against us, the judge dropped the one against me because I had taken Dustin to the meeting spot. However, if I did not physically remove my ten-year-old son from my car the next time, the court would surmise I had no control over my child and would take away my custody rights. In that event, Dustin would be placed in a boys' home.

As though that weren't enough, the judge seemed to be making my son out to be a spoiled brat and found him guilty of violating the visitation court order. He sentenced him to ten days in juvenile detention but suspended the ruling.

"Young man." The judge glared at Dustin. "If you miss another visitation, not only will I reverse the ten-day detention, but I will add additional days as I see fit."

And that was that. With the slamming of the gavel, my stomach clinched, and I wanted to throw up. I remember thinking, *Is this real life right now? Is this really happening?* How could this judge who just agreed to sign an order of protection against Greg then turn around and force my son to go with his abuser? Then to make matters worse, he warned Dustin with juvenile detention if he didn't spend time with his dad, the very one who abused him. I had promised my son that we would protect him and that everything would be okay. But, really, I felt like no one was protecting him. The court system had failed us.

I faced my son and cupped his face in my hands. "I'm so sorry. If I try to protect you, I'll lose you." We both stood there and cried.

Days after court, Dustin withdrew even more. The therapy sessions with his father were useless. Dustin refused to talk in front of his dad.

"Why should I?" he said after another failed session. "If I say anything, Dad will yell at me when I go to his house."

I never wanted my kids to experience the same heartbreak I'd felt growing up with my parents, and yet Dustin's words echoed my experience as a youth.

Cindy and Dustin fought more than usual. One morning she asked if it would be okay if she locked her bedroom door at night.

"No," I said. Her bedroom was upstairs. What if there was a fire?

"Mom, please."

"Why?"

She lowered her voice. "Dustin scares me. Several times in the middle of the night, I found him standing at the foot of my bed. He just stares at me, not saying a word."

Concern filled me. Could he be having the same thoughts toward his sister that he had toward his father? I asked Cindy to sit at the kitchen table.

"Dustin, please come here." Once he sat, I said, "Why do you stand at your sister's bed in the middle of the night?"

"I don't." He glared at Cindy.

"Liar!" she screamed across the table.

He yelled back at her.

Before the yelling could continue, I stopped them. "You're not allowed to leave this table until you work out whatever is going on between you. We're family. We only have each other. You two need to talk."

After a few minutes of arguing back and forth, Dustin screamed out, "I hate you because you wouldn't protect me!"

Shocked, I stood in the doorway and cried. Both of my children were crying as well.

Cindy looked at her brother and said, "Dustin, I am sorry. How could I protect you when I can't even protect myself?"

I sat with them and looked from Cindy to Dustin. "Your sister may be two years older than you, but she's not much bigger."

They were no longer screaming but talking. Cindy got up from the table and went over and hugged Dustin. His anger for his sister dissolved in that moment. But his other struggles were far from over.

Later, during a nightmare, Dustin experienced chest pains and shortness of breath. I reached out to his doctor, who set up an appointment with a cardiologist. Dustin had to wear a heart monitor for twenty-four hours straight. Afterward, the doctor diagnosed him with tachycardia—the medical term for a rapid heart rate. At one time, around 7:00 p.m., Dustin's heart rate jumped to 180 and measured even higher several times in the night when Dustin should have been asleep. I knew the time when his heart rate jumped because he'd talked to his dad on the phone around seven. A typical heart rate for a ten-year-old is 70–110. The doctor instructed me to check his pulse every hour and record it in a journal along with the time, what he was doing right before the measurement, and what and when he ate. We went back a week later for other tests. Doctors concluded the cause of his tachycardia was stress. I filled his therapist in on the tachycardia diagnosis, and she worked with Dustin on ways to relax and breathe when afraid or upset.

When I found out Dustin wasn't taking his pills, I asked for him to be taken off all his medications. He'd gotten into the habit of pretending to swallow, then hiding his pills everywhere. I even found some under the mulch in the flower beds where I went to plant flowers one morning. I already felt the medications were causing more harm than good when he did take them. Even with stopping medication, he continued therapy over the next year.

At times as I struggled to help Dustin, I lost my temper and felt out of control. By the end of the year, we were both in counseling. From the weight of everything I carried, I finally reached a point of desperation. My children were my only reason to live, but sometimes that reason wasn't enough. The negative recordings playing in my mind often persuaded me they deserved better. When I believed this, nothing could convince me otherwise.

I sat on my bed and dialed a suicide hotline. I cried uncontrollably, almost to the point of hyperventilation as the emotions over the past year flooded to the surface. I had been drowning in the guilt for not knowing what happened to my son. Beyond frustrated with the changes in his roller-coaster attitude and behavior, I felt completely helpless for not being able to protect him, convinced I had failed as a mother. The financial strain from attorney fees, medication, and counseling had taken its toll on my marriage. I couldn't talk to Charlie about any of it; he was neither supportive nor involved. I could no longer deal with anything. By the end of the phone call, I had agreed to return to therapy immediately.

CHAPTER 13

Blindsided

On September 12, 2005, another storm crashed into my life. One that almost ended with me being murdered in a Walmart parking lot.

My job consisted of stocking shelves from 2:00 p.m. until 11:00 p.m. After finishing one of my shifts, I clocked out, then picked up a few groceries. I grabbed the two bags I'd purchased and put my pocketbook on my left shoulder. The coolness in the air of the approaching fall was refreshing when I left the store. Employees were required to park at the end of the parking lot, but every night on my last break I moved my car closer to the storefront. I knew I wasn't supposed to, but I'd rather get in trouble for relocating my car than walk in the dark late at night by myself. My car was about the sixth one from the front doors. I proceeded to unlock my car when someone spoke to me from behind. I looked over my right shoulder while holding my keys in the door lock and was startled by a young man standing beside me.

"Excuse me, ma'am, can you tell me how to get to—"

Suddenly, he punched me in the face and grabbed for my pocketbook. He continued to punch me in the face, head, and the back of my shoulder as he knocked me to the ground. The strap on my purse had twisted around my shoulder, making it impossible for it to slide off. By this time the bags of groceries had ripped, and the contents were scattered over the ground.

A white pickup truck with a young girl about the same age as my attacker in the driver's seat blocked my car in its parking spot. The passenger door of the truck was open. With both hands on my pocketbook, the assailant pulled me and my purse toward the truck. He jumped in, and the driver began to pull away, dragging me to the ground. The strap finally broke, releasing me. Shocked and bruised, I sat up and noticed my cell phone close to me on the pavement. During the struggle it had fallen out of my pocketbook. I shook violently as I dialed 911.

"911 what is your emergency?" a woman said on the other end of the call.

Gulping back a sob I said, "I've been robbed. I, um . . ." I struggled to get my thoughts together.

"Ma'am, I need you to tell me what happened."

I closed my eyes, inhaled a shaky breath, and explained. I also gave the direction the truck had headed out of the parking lot.

After being reassured someone was on the way, I picked up the salvageable groceries while I waited for the police and ambulance. I thought I'd gathered everything but noticed one more item had fallen out of my pocketbook—an envelope. With bruised and bleeding hands I picked it up. I'd gotten paid the night before and cashed my paycheck on the way to work but hadn't had enough time to place the money inside my wallet. The envelope held all my cash. Amazed at how two of the most important items I needed had fallen out of my pocketbook, I could only contribute what I'd found to the hand of God.

After placing the groceries inside my car, I walked to the front doors of the store to wait for the police. As I approached, a fellow employee, obviously on break, leaned against the wall smoking a cigarette. We briefly made eye contact before he turned his head. I knew he had witnessed the whole event but did nothing to help me. Before the incident, we had spoken on many occasions, but afterward he never made eye contact or spoke to me again.

The police arrived, and I told them what I could, but I didn't feel like I offered much help. I had only caught a glimpse of my assailant. Everything happened so fast, but, at the same time, it felt like the moment lasted forever. One thing kept eating at me, though: there was something about his eyes.

I was taken to the hospital, cleaned up, and photographed. My body suffered most of the attack on my right side. My face was badly bruised, and my eye was swollen almost completely shut. Knots raised about half an inch on my forehead, under my eye, and the right side of my jaw. A golf ball–sized knot appeared on my shoulder. My forearm was bruised along with scrapes and bruises on both knees. When the hospital finished my examination after 2:00 a.m., I dreaded calling home to ask my husband to pick me up. The first time I called no one answered. I hung up and tried again. This time fifteen-year-old Cindy answered the phone.

"Why are you calling in the middle of the night? Aren't you supposed to be home?" She yawned through the receiver.

"Wake up Charlie."

"What's wrong?" The sound of sleep disappeared from her voice.

"I've been attacked and robbed." I knew she heard the quiver in my voice. "Wake up Charlie. I need him to pick me up at the hospital."

Thirty minutes later Charlie stormed into the emergency room. His anger grew as I explained what happened.

"Someone's going to pay for what they did to you."

In a full rage, Charlie wanted to kill somebody, which was the reason I had dreaded calling him. He demanded to see the surveillance footage from Walmart's parking lot. I knew the only reason he wanted to see it was to see what my assailant looked like in hopes of finding him before the police did.

He drove me home without seeing the footage, silent the entire way. I understood his silence because I'd been with my husband long enough to know he didn't handle stressful situations well and needed time to process.

We arrived home around 3:30 a.m. Cindy had waited up to see for herself if I was okay. When I walked into the house, my daughter took one look at me and burst into tears. Charlie went straight to bed, and not long after him, Cindy went to her room. I sat on the couch as my stomach churned, and my entire body still shook from the adrenaline of the attack. Knowing I wouldn't sleep, I called the credit card companies to report the robbery. One of the credit cards had already been used to purchase gas at a 7-Eleven only fifteen minutes after the attack. Another purchase had been made at a McDonald's in a neighboring town. I guessed my attacker had worked up an appetite after beating and robbing me.

The thieves had used my credit cards while I was in the hospital; the detectives had a lead on their direction and possible video footage from the establishments. Unfortunately, neither 7-Eleven nor McDonald's had surveillance cameras.

When the time came to wake the boys to get ready for school, I knew there would be no disguising my appearance from thirteen-year-old Dustin and seven-year-old Charles. Their shocked expression revealed disbelief and fear at the sight of my face. To protect Dustin from the truth—I'd once again been beaten by a man—I lied.

"It's okay." I tried to turn more of the left side of my face in their direction. "A box fell and hit me in the face."

Both boys openly wept. As Dustin watched me, his distressed expression turned to one of fury. He didn't believe me for even a second. Because he'd seen bruising on me before, he knew someone had hit me.

"Was it Charlie?" Dustin asked.

I had to tell them the truth. If I didn't, Dustin would blame his stepdad. I looked from one brother to the other. "No, he didn't do this. I was assaulted by someone who robbed me." I held Dustin's gaze until I felt he believed me.

After the boys left for school, Charlie drove me to Walmart to get my car and meet with the police to view the surveillance footage. Disappointed neither 7-Eleven nor McDonald's had video footage of the attack, I'd hoped the cameras at Walmart would reveal a license tag number or a visual of their appearance. Wrong again.

The footage showed a small pickup truck sitting in the fire lane beside the front door. A customer walked from the parking lot toward the store entrance by herself. The passenger door of the truck slowly opened then closed when someone else appeared. A few moments later I walked out. The truck followed behind me until I reached my car. When the truck stopped, the assailant emerged, leaving his passenger door open. I witnessed my attack on the video—the beating, being dragged, and lying on the pavement. The poor quality of the tape prevented anyone from seeing what any of us looked like, but the most gut-wrenching part, we never saw a tag number. The uselessness of the video put us back to square one. One thing I noticed in the footage was at least six people parked and exited their cars within eyesight of my attack.

Not one person called 911 or told anyone inside the store what was taking place. No one helped me, again.

The detective working on the case called my cell one evening to ask if I was at home.

"No, I'm at my son's football game." I covered my other ear to shut out some of the noise.

"Okay, meet me at the gate during halftime," Detective Hayden said.

When halftime arrived, Charlie and I walked down to one of the school buildings to stand under the lights.

"I need you to look at these." Detective Hayden handed me a photo lineup.

Sweat dripped down the nape of my neck, my hands shook, and my heart pounded so hard I thought it would explode. "I don't know if I can."

What if I couldn't remember what he looked like?

"Take a deep breath, Mrs. Collier. Take your time."

I wish he'd told me to sit down. I took a deep breath and opened the file folder. There were ten to twelve pictures on the paper. Immediately, one of them jumped out at me. My knees gave way, I dropped to the ground, and I struggled to breathe. I looked up at Detective Hayden and, through tears and with trembling hands, pointed to one of the pictures. Without any doubt I knew it was him.

"Are you absolutely sure?"

"Yes."

He retrieved the photo. "I'm proud of you. I know this was hard, but you did well."

He also informed me the woman driving the truck had called her estranged husband the same night and told him she and her boyfriend had robbed a woman at the Bedford Walmart and were headed to Philadelphia. He called the Bedford police department and reported their crime.

Warrants were issued for their arrests and the Philadelphia police were notified. On September 17, 2005, the Bedford police department received a phone call stating both assailants had been arrested in Philadelphia and were awaiting extradition. Detective Hayden was on his way to pick them up. A sense of relief washed over me knowing my attacker was behind bars and the whole ordeal would soon to be over. No longer would I have to look over my shoulder fearing he could find and hurt me again.

But the next call from Detective Hayden took away every ounce of safety I'd experienced hours earlier.

"Mrs. Collier, I hate to inform you, but there was a mix up in paperwork in Philly. By the time we got here, the department had to release one of the suspects. I'm sorry."

I gripped the phone receiver in silence.

"We'll find him. We have his girlfriend in custody, and she's agreed to help locate him in exchange for a lighter sentence. Don't worry." After a long silence, he said again, "Please don't worry."

I hung up, then stumbled outside to sit alone with my thoughts, which raced with increasing fear. Turns out, I wasn't the only person he'd attacked but the third. The same day he assaulted me, he had beaten and robbed another woman in a different Walmart parking lot. For whatever reason she had refused to press charges. In a grocery store parking lot, he had attempted to rob an elderly man at gun point, but when the man defended himself with his cane, the thief fled. Then he found and attacked me. I had picked him out of a photo lineup and was the only willing to testify. I stood between him and his freedom. He knew where I worked and where I lived—my driver's license gave him my home address.

Following the issue of the warrants, I was contacted by the local newspaper to be interviewed about the incident. I learned the man who had attacked and robbed me had been released from prison two months prior. At the age of fifteen he had bludgeoned a sixty-three-year-old man to death and spent just shy of ten years in prison with ten years suspended.

My anxiety rose to a whole new level. He knew I had pressed charges. He also knew, if convicted, he would serve the ten years of his suspended sentence. Over the next nine months I experienced a kind of fear unlike any I'd experienced before. I didn't sleep due to nightmares and the fear that he'd come after me during the night.

I returned to work after my face healed enough for makeup to hide the bruises. My supervisor allowed me to change my shift to daytime hours due to my level of anxiety of leaving work late at night. Until my assailant was found, he also felt it would be safer for me to work during the day when the store was busier. The attacker's mug shot hung beside the time clock and in the breakroom. I appreciated the store's effort, but seeing his picture every day made me uncomfortable and was a constant reminder my attacker was still on the run.

Sometimes on break I caught myself staring at his face. There was something in my gut that kept bringing me back to his eyes. Before I did the photo lineup, I was concerned I wouldn't be able to remember what he looked like because everything happened so fast, yet his picture jumped off the page in the lineup because of his eyes. In the breakroom, when I'd regained my composure, I would purposely look at his eyes again to see what stood out. I didn't see anything, but I *knew* I'd seen something in his eyes. On a day while I stared at his picture again, I had a flashback of that night.

"Excuse me, miss," he'd said.

I had turned to look at him, and we'd made eye contact.

Immediately, I knew he was going to hurt me. In an instant, I saw it in his eyes. I knew the look, having witnessed it almost every time I'd faced a severe physical or sexual attack. There's something about the pupils. I don't know if I've seen the devil or sense evil in all my abuser's eyes, but I do know without a shadow of a doubt, I get a sense I am in harm's way when I make eye contact with them.

After the attack, I changed my hair color and style, trying to convince myself he wouldn't recognize me. I continued to struggle at work with the constant fear. On many occasions if a customer startled me, I had panic attacks and trouble breathing. I would break out in a sweat and shake uncontrollably, unable to speak until I regained control of my emotions.

During this whole experience not once did I have the *why me* mentality. I thought *Of course me. How could it not be me? Why would it not be me?* I wondered what could possibly be left in my life to destroy.

Six months after my attack, the girlfriend, also the driver of the getaway vehicle, was convicted for her part in the crime and sentenced to serve two years in jail. During her sentencing I sat in the courtroom and listened to her cry for lenience to the judge because her two small children needed their mother. *Are you kidding me?*

The commonwealth attorney asked, "Do you think about Mrs. Collier's three children and how this could have very easily been a murder trial right now instead of an assault and robbery trial had the strap on her purse not broken? Do you realize your decision to drive off while dragging Mrs. Collier on the ground next to the truck could have ended her life?"

She replied, "I didn't care about her or her kids, I only cared about getting money to get high."

Ten months after the assault, I received a phone call from Detective Hayden letting me know my attacker had been apprehended in a nearby town. I'd convinced myself this day would never come, and yet it had. With a heavy weight instantly lifted off me, I cried tears of relief. But the process was far from over.

Twice his sentencing date was moved. Once because he didn't like his attorney, the second time because he had been put on an anxiety medication due to being depressed at the thought of going back to prison where he previously was abused. His attorney claimed he was too mentally unstable to appear in court. When we did have the sentencing hearing, I sat in the courtroom again and listened to how everyone should feel sorry for this individual because of his rough life in prison.

My anger boiled as I listened to their excuses. Did they expect me to feel sorry when the female driver begged for leniency because of her two small children? And now feel sorry for a man who'd chosen to bludgeon another person to death, then claim he faced anxiety from being abused in prison? Yet two months after he'd been released, he held a man at gun point, attempted to rob him after he had already robbed someone else, then beat and robbed me. And now I'm supposed to believe *he's* suffering from depression at the thought of returning to prison? What about the emotional trauma I, my husband, and my children had been put through daily for a year and a half because of the whole ordeal? What about the consequences for what this man and woman did? I sat through both of their sentencings disgusted at their self-pity and lack of remorse.

One year and seven months after I almost lost my life, the robber was sentenced to a total of twenty years in the penitentiary without parole—fifteen years for the robbery, two for the attempted robbery, and a mandatory three for the use of a firearm in commission of a felony from earlier during the same night. On top of the twenty-year sentence, he had the suspended ten-year portion of his previous murder conviction reinstated for violating probation.

Justice. For the first time in my life one of my abusers was held accountable.

CHAPTER 14

Message from Above

In the midst of everything else going on in my life, Charlie left me. We'd not gotten into a huge fight, yet he left. In fact, my daughter—now a freshman in college and living on campus—called me at work and wanted to know why Charlie had moved out.

"What?" I gripped the receiver tighter.

"Yeah, he texted me and said he'd moved back home with his parents."

"Why?" My mind raced.

"He didn't say."

Confused, I replied, "You must have misunderstood him."

"I don't think so, Mom. I just thought you should know."

After hanging up I returned to work, but my focus had remained on the conversation with Cindy. When I returned home, I found most of Charlie's stuff was gone. I checked the balance of our joint bank account to find he'd taken out all the money. Anger raged through me. It was the end of the week, how was I going to buy groceries? How would I feed the boys? I didn't make enough cleaning for a couple days to cover our living expenses.

When two of the people I cleaned for found out what had happened, they made sure we had more than enough food and helped cover my bills for a month. I was extremely grateful for their kindness and generosity. They truly blessed me. Soon I was blessed again with a full-time job cleaning condos. With a full-time and part-time job, I knew we'd be okay, at least financially.

Charlie continued to pay my rent and car payment. We agreed Charles would live with me but could stay with his father anytime he wanted. The problems in our marriage had been between his father and me. Charlie had left me, not his son.

I wasn't surprised he'd left, even though the timing of his leaving caught me off guard. Subconsciously, I had known it was bound to happen. We'd had a way of bringing out the worst in each other. More than five months elapsed before I realized his decision gave me something I never expected. A new chance at life.

Because he'd left, I hit rock bottom and was forced to deal with my past. For the first time I was held accountable for how I'd dealt with the scars I carried. Facing my past and finding forgiveness were the hardest things I'd ever done but also the most rewarding. I finally had peace and hope for my future, a future beyond the scars. Something I never dreamed possible.

People seem to show up at times in my life when I need help the most. Even though I became a Christian in my youth, I believed God had abandoned me when I faced devastating trauma. And why not? Everyone else had deserted me. In my mind, God had allowed me to experience so much pain and suffering and still would not let me die. I knew without a doubt, God had turned his back on me. I had no problem turning my back on Him.

I discovered when I reached the end of my rope—hanging on by the last thread—that God had not left me but had sent messages of encouragement that impacted my life in a huge way. Being so hurt and angry, I almost missed the messages God sent to help facilitate my healing.

The first messenger, a woman named Sam, came into my life two weeks before my attempted suicide in the bathroom from chapter 1.

God knew my husband was going to leave me, and I was no longer strong enough to get through it. I started working for her the week before Charlie left.

God sent me Sam.

I connected with Sam through another woman I'd cleaned for. They went to the same church, and she gave me her friend's phone number. Sam and her husband had been trying to sell their house and wanted someone to help with the cleaning.

We immediately connected, and I felt a sense of peace around her. While I cleaned, she talked to me about my faith and managed to quote verses from the Bible at the exact time I needed to be encouraged. She read scriptures to me and answered questions I didn't even express out loud. I believed God was speaking to me through her.

Sam made sure I had money to pay my bills and buy enough food for the kids on a regular basis. She knew I was going through a difficult time.

One day while cleaning, Sam asked me to join her and her husband in the living room. After I sat, she looked at the cuff of my long-sleeved shirt.

"Did you try to hurt yourself?" She raised her eyes to meet mine.

Without looking down, I tugged at the bottom of my sleeve to cover the bandage. I knew she'd seen it. I burst into tears.

Sam hugged me. "Amy, God is with you, but you need to trust Him. Pushing Him away isn't the answer."

I knew what she said was true, but I didn't know how to trust anyone.

"May we pray for you?"

We held hands as Sam and her husband prayed. She asked God to show His presence and comfort me. Before I headed home, she wrote these words on a piece of paper and gave it to me, "I can do all things through Christ who strengthens me."

Sam was persistent in her encouragement for me to turn back to God. Because of her, I wanted to rekindle my relationship with Him. I found the strength I needed to read my Bible and pray again. Within two months of our first meeting, Sam's house was sold, and she and her husband left the state.

Our last time together, Sam hugged me. "It took longer than we wanted for our house to sell, but that's okay." She smiled. "God had His reason."

As soon as she said those words, I knew *I* was the reason. God used Sam to help bring me closer to Him. I'm so grateful to God for bringing us together. God wasn't done reminding me of His presence in my life.

After an extremely stressful and draining week working full-time as a housekeeper at a popular vacation resort on the lake near my home, I wanted the day to be over. I worked five days a week, eight to ten hours a day, and on my two days off, I cleaned private homes. I approached the next condo on my list and knocked on the door.

"Housekeeping." I assumed with the beautiful weather outside no one would be in. The bright sunny day carried the sounds of boats coming in and out with children laughing and playing at the pool.

When no one responded from inside the condo, I unlocked the door and called again, "Housekeeping."

Still no response. Propping the door open, I stepped inside to collect the dirty bath towels. The unit was a smaller one with two bedrooms, two baths, a full kitchen, and a living room.

As I walked toward the first bathroom, I heard a faint voice.

"Hello, can you help me?"

I jumped. I hated when someone surprised me. I made my way through the condo and noticed the sliding glass door in the living room leading onto the balcony was open. As I drew closer, I heard an elderly woman's voice.

"Is anyone there? Can you help me?"

"Yes, ma'am, it's housekeeping," I said.

In a soft, sweet voice she asked, "Can you bring me a bottle of water from the refrigerator and my cane? I can't get up. I'm in a wheelchair."

"Yes, ma'am." I scanned the room and found her cane leaning against the living room wall opposite the balcony door. I retrieved a bottle of water from the refrigerator and picked up the cane on my way outside. A woman with silver hair and glasses sat in a wheelchair. She appeared to be in her late seventies.

When she looked up at me, her eyes widened, and she opened her mouth as though to speak but said nothing. I froze at her expression, not sure what to do next.

After a few seconds of silence, which seemed like an eternity, she said, "They're so beautiful. Come closer to me." Tears filled her eyes.

I didn't know what to say or do, but for some reason, I walked toward her, gripping her cane and the bottle of water in my shaky hands. I set the bottle on a small table beside her wheelchair and leaned the cane against the table. As I took a step back, she leaned forward, keeping her eyes on me. There was a softness in them that seemed to see straight through to my soul. I didn't understand why I wasn't afraid of the way she'd focused on me.

She reached for my hand. "You're surrounded by angels; you're not alone. I don't know what you're going through, but God brought me here so I could tell you."

Chills ran through my body, and the hairs stood up on my skin. Immediately tears filled my eyes. *Don't cry, don't you cry*, I repeated silently to myself.

I tugged at the bottom of my long-sleeve shirt that covered the bandages wrapped around my wrist. My mind returned to two days earlier, when I had sat on my bathroom floor crying, feeling alone, and hopeless. I'd yelled at God as I sliced through my skin. Where was He and why wouldn't He protect me from all the pain I'd lived with for such a long time? Could God have brought this stranger into my life to show me He did care? That I wasn't alone?

She pulled me out of my thoughts when she asked, "May I hug you?"

A lump had formed in my throat. "Sure." I tried hard not to burst into tears. Swallowing, I stepped closer and bent to hug her. A calming peace ran through my body as she wrapped her arms around me. It was like nothing I'd ever experienced before. When she let me go, she seemed to study me.

"Will you please sit with me for a few minutes? You don't have to clean. I'll tell them you did a great job, so you won't get into trouble. Please sit, being close to you and your angels makes me feel like I'm closer to God," she said.

Really it was the other way around; I felt closer to God in her presence. "Okay," I said.

As I sat in the chair beside her, I didn't want to leave any more than she wanted me to. Had she really seen angels around me? Was she an angel? Did God send her to let me know He was with me? Was I losing my mind? Whatever the reason, as I sat on that balcony with her, I experienced peace. More than anything else I felt closer to God.

"I came to attend a class reunion. Imagine folks my age still having reunions. There aren't too many of us left." She shook her head. "Didn't want to come."

She told me her health wasn't good and she really couldn't afford the trip, but her daughter and son-in-law had traveled with her.

Looking out over the lake, she continued, "I wanted to get some fresh air, so my daughter helped me get outside. Before taking off for the day, they forgot to leave me with my cane." She chuckled. "I can't go anywhere without it. Not even back inside. I was mighty parched. Thank you for the water." She reached for the cold bottle and had a long drink. "So many times, I wanted to cancel the trip, but something kept stopping me. Something kept telling me it was important to come. As soon as I saw you, I knew God had sent me here to give you His message," she explained. "I have something I want you to have." She reached for a Bible sitting on the small table beside her wheelchair. She pulled out a bookmark, then wrote something on the side. She smiled as she handed it to me.

I can do all things through Christ who strengthens me. These were the same words Sam had given me two days before. Without a doubt, I knew God was trying to get my attention. Stunned at seeing the verse again, I struggled to process what was happening.

I thanked the kind woman for the bookmark and told her I needed to get back to work before someone came looking for me. Entering the hallway, I knew God had answered my questions. I pushed my cleaning cart toward the elevator and looked up to the ceiling.

"You have my attention. I'm listening, and I'm sorry for thinking You turned Your back on me. I do believe You're with me." A calmness overcame me. My healing process began when I realized God would be with me. I was not alone. I was never alone.

I smiled.

CHAPTER 15

Learning to Live Again

What now? Where do I go from here? What if I'm too broken? Why should this time be any different?

Throughout my thirty-seven years, I'd spent ten in and out of therapy. Many sessions ended with me drenched in sweat, my eyes swollen, and feeling more broken and damaged than when I'd arrived. Parts of my past I couldn't revisit—I did not want to revisit—because of fear. Yet a greater fear was that my therapist wouldn't be *able* to help me.

My last therapist said, "Amy, I feel it's best if we stop trying to go back into your past and start concentrating on your future. I can see trying to bring up repressed memories is causing you too much harm."

Thank you, God. Finally, there would be no more pressure to talk about my buried past. I could breathe. This therapist told me to read books on positive thoughts and gratitude. "Let's try this direction," he said.

I purchased a book at a local bookstore. At first it gave me hope, but soon the familiar negative voices took over again. Still, the conversation with the therapist continued to tug at me: *It's best if we stop trying to go back into your past.* Maybe I'd given up too soon. Maybe healing needed to start with my damaging thoughts. I knew there would never be a quick fix. The process would take a lot of work, but I'd made a commitment to my children to get well, and I couldn't let them or myself down. I needed to develop an awareness of how I responded to triggers. I had to give everything I could to reprogram my mind.

Not long after Sam moved away and I'd met the elderly woman at the condo, I met a new client, Donalyn. Like Sam, she was not aware of my struggles or my past, but she would talk to me about a scripture or part of a sermon. Her words were what I needed to hear.

I eventually shared about my past with Donalyn. She prayed with me and for me. Her encouragement gave me hope. One day as I worked, I talked with Donalyn about my children. I will never forget what she said.

"Amy, look at how wonderful your three children turned out. If you really were all those things you have convinced yourself that you are, then how did they turn out to be as wonderful as they are?"

I stood there, lost for words. My mind searched for an answer to prove I was a bad mother. But this time the negative recordings that usually worked toward my destruction didn't have a chance of winning. I went back to cleaning and considered Donalyn's words. *Wow, I never looked at my children as something I had done right.* My world had been so consumed with self-loathing and blame that I couldn't see the positive things in my life.

Cindy, Dustin, and Charles were good students. At fourteen, my daughter knew what she wanted to be when she grew up. At sixteen, she joined the junior rescue squad and then the fire department. In college, she made the dean's list and worked toward her degree in the medical field.

As a junior in high school, Dustin played football and wrestled. He had wrestled from the age of six and made it to the state tournament his junior year. I couldn't remember a day when he didn't tell me how much he loved me and regularly gave me hugs and kisses. Attuned to when something bothered me, he would stay with me until he was sure I was okay.

My youngest son was eleven, going on twenty, a naturally gifted athlete both in baseball and wrestling. He set goals and worked hard to achieve them. Even though he was not brought up in the church, his Bible was never far from his side. His faith was incredibly strong, and it showed in his actions. He honored and praised God with every accomplishment, and I admired him for that and often wondered where he got his courage from.

My life had revolved around my children. They were my shield, and I felt safest with them. Even with all three playing multiple sports throughout childhood, I sat in the bleachers by myself. I never initiated conversations with the other mothers. It wasn't that I didn't want to talk to them. I felt like they wouldn't want to talk to me.

All my children were strong and driven. They knew what they wanted and had unshakeable confidence. They were everything I wished I could have been, but I never once looked at them as a reflection of how I had mothered. How could I not want to do everything I could to get better? I wanted them to be as proud of me as I was of them.

With a new determination of not giving up, I made a trip to the local bookstore again. I read inside and back covers in the self-help section, searching for anything resembling my history of abuse and for something to give me hope. I picked out a couple of books and a notebook hoping to find a way to understand and change the way I thought. Every free minute I had, I read. I kept the notebook with me so when something jumped off the page to inspire me or give me hope or encouragement, I wrote it down. My notebook became an extension of myself like a security blanket or my newest weapon for my troubling thoughts. I carried it with me because I never knew when something would trigger a memory or turn on the negative recordings and cause me to break down. When the negative thoughts came, I'd open my notebook and read out loud until the recordings in my head stopped and I could control my tears. Afterward, I'd return to whatever I was doing. This became my daily routine. With each avoided breakdown, I felt a little stronger and more confident. Gradually, it became easier to quiet the negative recordings.

I grew in my awareness of the power of thoughts. One positive thought brought a smile to my face and a feeling of encouragement. A bad one brought tears and filled me with doubt and sadness. I continued to remind myself I could control my thoughts and how I let them affect me. A lack of awareness could easily cause me to slip back to what was familiar.

I also recognized I needed restoration in my soul. I struggled with my faith between the teachings I'd received growing up and my belief that God only wanted to punish me. My feelings of anger and abandonment kept me from seeing the truth. Sometimes the confusion and uncertainty were overwhelming. I never denied the existence of God. I believed he answered prayers, just not mine.

My eyes were opened when I acknowledged God's constant presence in my life. I grappled with my emotions and questioned my abilities to move forward. Sometimes when I wanted to run away with no set destination, I often ended up in a random church parking lot where I'd scream and cry to God. On one such escape,

God met me in the parking lot. When I pulled in, I let it all out. I cried and questioned God. I told Him I didn't understand why He had abandoned me when I was a child. I needed Him, I still needed Him, and I couldn't do this alone anymore.

When I calmed down and became quiet, God showed through flashbacks from my past that He had heard my cries.

At thirteen when Mr. Johnson was on top of me, touching me, I'd prayed for God to save me. Then the baby cried. For the first time I no longer felt fear as I remembered the episode but rather awareness that God had answered my prayer. If that baby had not cried, Mr. Johnson would not have stopped. The outcome of the situation would have ended in a more traumatic way.

The next image showed me at sixteen when Roger raped me. I remembered my thoughts. *Is the giant going to rape me too? Are they going to kill me? Surely, Roger is not going to take a chance on going back to jail.* Then there was the loud knock on the door, and the giant yelled someone was coming. Again, I didn't feel the fear and shame my flashbacks often caused but instead knew it had been God who had caused these men to return me home alive.

A final flashback showed me lying on my living room floor during a fight with Greg. I felt myself losing consciousness. My daughter cried in my ear, "Mommy." A burst of strength rushed through me. Deep down I instantly knew where the strength had come from.

How could I have been so blind to His presence?

As the tears ran down my face, I had a long talk with God. I told Him I was sorry for all the years of screaming at Him and asked forgiveness for ever doubting His presence.

When I needed Him most, He was there. He had not abandoned me. Some of the abuse I suffered, as bad as it was, could have been worse had He not been with me. God didn't force control on the choices I made, situations I put myself in, or the evil in the hearts of the abusers, but He was present and did prevent far harsher outcomes.

When I returned home from the church parking lot, I picked up my Bible and opened my heart. Several days later Donalyn gave me my first book of devotions. I set aside thirty minutes every day to work on rebuilding my faith through immersing myself in God's Word.

As I learned how to change my way of thinking, my whole world changed too. I became aware of how my thoughts in the present were becoming different from my thinking in the past.

The best way to describe my revelation is through a metaphor. In the past, I felt like a misfit toy inside a toy box, convinced no one wanted to play with the only broken toy. But in reality, I'd hidden from everyone and never allowed anyone to play with me. It was easier to remain inside the toy box in protection mode than to take a chance of being hurt or rejected. This had become my way of life.

The truth was, even if I tried, I couldn't let love in. I pushed everyone away. It didn't matter how much anyone said they loved me. I believed I was unlovable. I thought my brokenness would cause those who loved me to be broken as well.

I carried the guilt and shame from my childhood experiences in isolation. Staying silent no matter what was ingrained in me, and that led me to believe I brought all the years of abuse on myself. People hurt me because I was the screw up. The monster my own mother didn't want. Why would I dare think I was worthy enough for anyone else to want to be a part of my life? I stayed isolated in my pain-filled world.

But that was about to change.

As my eyes were opened, I became more aware of how I related to the outside world. I could see my life from the outside looking in, instead of the inside looking out. Rather than being consumed by my emotions, I observed my past actions and how I responded. This knowledge gave me what I needed on my road to recovery.

I finally realized the cycle in which I had spent my life suffering from so much abuse had caused me to carry around anger, hate, guilt, shame, sadness, and mistrust. The memories caused me to withdraw inside myself and never let anyone get close. I'd felt isolated and alone. These emotions, in turn, caused the people who truly did love me to express sadness, helplessness, and anger on my behalf. Then the cycle would repeat. When I became aware of the cycle, I promised myself I would do everything I could to break it. I had made progress and knew I was moving in the right direction.

I may never know the depths of pain I caused those closest to me. For that I am truly sorry.

CHAPTER 16

Forgiveness

I'd made progress on quieting the negative voices, but the pain remained. I felt stuck. In the past when I reached this point I gave into the pain and sunk back into the darkness of depression, but this time giving up was not an option.

I prayed. "Father, you have my attention. I know I'm not alone, and You are with me. Father, I'm lost. I ask You to show me how to move forward. Please help me to heal. Amen."

Over the next couple of weeks, everything I picked up to read had something to do with forgiveness, including my daily devotionals. I skipped over sections about forgiveness, having no desire to read anything on the topic. I cringed at the thought of forgiving the people who had hurt me and caused so much pain. How could forgiving my abusers help me heal? Had the authors of the books I read been molested, raped, beaten, verbally abused, or abandoned? Even if they had, the thought of forgiving was absurd to me. I thought forgiving someone meant I would agree with what they did to me, that I condoned their actions. With every ounce of my being, I hated my abusers. I hated them because they were not sorry. I hated them for taking years away from me. They did not deserve my forgiveness, and it would be insane to let them off the hook.

Needing to forgive continued to tug at my heart. The topic continued to pop up everywhere. I did *not* want to hear about forgiveness. I knew God whispered into my spirit, *You asked for help, and you asked for healing. But you refuse to listen.* I didn't want to forgive, but I half-heartedly went back to my reading material I'd intentionally skipped. It did not take me long to realize everything I'd thought about forgiveness was false.

I began to study the meaning, and this is what I learned: "Forgiveness is the intentional and voluntary process by which a victim undergoes a change in feelings and attitude regarding an offense, lets go of negative emotions such as vengefulness, with an increased ability to wish the offender well. Forgiveness is different from condoning. . . . It is not excusing . . . , not forgetting . . . , and not reconciliation."[1]

> In general, [forgiveness] involves an intentional decision to let go of resentment and anger.
>
> The act that hurt or offended you might always be with you. But working on forgiveness can lessen that act's grip on you. It can help free you from the control of the person who harmed you. Sometimes, forgiveness might even lead to feelings of understanding, empathy and compassion for the one who hurt you.
>
> Forgiveness doesn't mean forgetting or excusing the harm done to you. It also doesn't necessarily mean making up with the person who caused the harm.

---

1. "The Power of Forgiveness," People Builders, https://www.peoplebuilders .com.au/blog/the-power-of-forgiveness#:~:text=Forgiveness%20is%20the%20 intentional%20and,to%20wish%20the%20offender%20well.

> Forgiveness brings a kind of peace that allows you to
> focus on yourself and helps you go on with life.[2]

I had to go back and reread that several times.

I realized the anger, fear, and hate I continued to carry in my heart were preventing me from moving forward and healing. Nothing could ever take back what had been done to me, but continuing to relive the events only punished me, not those who'd hurt me. My abusers would never feel sorry, but I needed to let go of the pain.

I wanted peace; I wanted to allow myself to feel love. To let go of the pain, I needed to let go of the past, and the only way to let go was to forgive. I had to close those chapters in my life in order to move forward. Even though I knew what needed to be done, my heart filled with anguish. Reading about forgiveness was so much easier than applying it. I understood forgiving was not condoning, excusing, or forgetting, but why was the idea still hard, and why did it cause me so much fear?

My abusers were not the only people I needed to forgive. They caused the initial pain, but I had allowed the pain to consume and control me by focusing on how much I hurt. I blamed myself for allowing the wound to remain open and grow deeper. I'd shut down and built walls, pushing everyone away as I created the lonely world in which I hid. I carried around as much anger and hate toward myself as I did to others. No one on earth hated

---

2. Mayo Clinic Staff, "Forgiveness: Letting Go of Grudges and Bitterness," Mayo Clinic, https://www.mayoclinic.org/healthy-lifestyle/adult-health /in-depth/forgiveness/art-20047692.

me more than I hated myself, nor was there a person on earth I hated more.

I wanted God to forgive me for all the hurt I'd caused the people who tried to love me and for the anguish I caused myself. I needed God to forgive me for all the cruel words I yelled at Him over many years. I really wanted to be set free, but I believed I deserved to be forgiven no more than I believed my abusers should be.

I had a conversation with Donalyn about my struggle. Without hesitation she looked me straight in the eyes and said, "If Jesus could ask His father to forgive His abusers and murderers as He was dying on the cross, how could you think you don't deserve to be forgiven? You can't control what has happened to you or how it affected your past decisions, but you can control what you do about it today."

I don't think Donalyn realizes how much God has used her in my healing process.

Over the next couple of days her words continued to run through my mind, and then it hit me. The fear and emotional turmoil I struggled with had more to do with the thought of letting go of my past than forgiveness. Letting go meant I would have to tear down my wall of protection and step out into an unknown way of dealing with life. If I got hurt again, where would I hide? How would I be able to protect myself? I'd always lived by shutting up, shutting down, and hiding. My past helped remind me what I needed to do to protect myself. My past was my identity; it was who I'd always been. The thought of letting go of my past sent terror and panic throughout my entire body. I dropped to my knees and cried out, "Lord, please give me strength. I want to run and hide so bad. I can't deal with the thought of the unfamiliar. I'm scared. I can't do this without You."

Deep down something told me to open my book of quotes. As I opened a random page, I read, "Trust in the LORD with all your heart and lean not on your own understanding" (Proverbs 3:5 NIV). Immediately calmness came over me. I repeated the verse every single time fear and doubt crept in. There were some days I repeated the verse nonstop from the time I woke up until I went to bed. I had to believe. I had to trust in faith. I didn't have a choice if I wanted to release myself from the internal prison where I'd spent more than two and a half decades of my life.

The week before Thanksgiving, and what would have been my wedding anniversary had my husband and I not split up, I went for a drive on back country roads to clear my mind. The myriad thoughts running through my mind made eating and sleeping impossible. After about thirty minutes, I pulled into an empty parking lot of an old church. I prayed. "God, I know I haven't forgiven those who hurt me, including myself, but I don't know how to. My past pain and memories continue to haunt me. I need Your help. Please show me how to forgive."

As I sobbed, I went down the list of abusers in my life. I spoke their names and what they'd done to me. I forgave them and would no longer allow the memory of their actions to keep me captive. I forgave myself for holding onto past hurts and for not allowing anyone to get close to me. I forgave myself for the anger, hate, resentment, shame, and blame I carried in my heart.

As I prayed, the tightness in my chest released its grip, and the fear and anger I had carried around for so long subsided. My abusers no longer had power over me. My memories no longer paralyzed me. A welcome, unknown feeling of peace filled me— something I had not believed I could experience. I felt stronger and lighter. I sat in the parking lot and thought about my life. I viewed things from a new perspective and immediately knew I was going to be okay. I could have a life beyond the scars.

During the next week some of the people I worked with and some of my employers commented there was something different about me. I smiled. A couple days later my husband called and asked if it would be okay if he came over to spend Thanksgiving dinner with the kids. To his surprise, I said yes.

Prior to my time with God in the parking lot, I hated Charlie for leaving. When he left, I was completely caught off guard. After Thanksgiving dinner, I told my estranged husband I forgave him for the pain he was responsible for throughout our years together. I did not blame him for leaving but thanked him and explained why.

"I wish you could know the person I am now." I looked into his eyes. "I'm sorry for never allowing you to love me or even get close to me. I'm sorry for not being the wife you deserved. I want to be the wife you hope to find one day."

He took hold of my hand. "I think I just found her."

We've been together ever since and have become best friends. I still have a long way to go—healing is a process. But I know I am on the right path. I've been given a second chance at life and now have hope. Something I didn't think possible.

CHAPTER 17

Saying Goodbye

My stepdad died at the age of fifty-three. He had been a part of my life for twenty-six years, and I struggled with his death for a long time. My stepdad was only thirteen years older than me. With the closeness in my age to him, I didn't think of him as a father figure. We had often talked on the phone, and he was the only reason I even considered visiting my mom's house. I could talk to him about anything and knew in my heart, no matter what, he had my back even when he felt I was in the wrong. He played an important role in my life, and I never questioned his love. To have him in my corner meant the world to me.

My stepdad had battled hepatitis C and cirrhosis of the liver for a handful of years. He'd lost a lot of weight and his skin color turned gray, but he continued to work and care for the house, yard, and my mom.

Once when Charlie (yes, my stepdad and my husband shared the same name) went to the doctor, they sent him to a hospital forty-five minutes away. Finding a mass on his liver, the doctor admitted him for a biopsy. Over the years when Charlie was hospitalized, I would go and sit with him while Mom went home to shower and feed her cats. But when he had his biopsy, I knew something was different.

When I walked into his hospital room and looked at him, I immediately sensed he wouldn't be with me much longer. My heart felt heavy, and tears threatened to spill down my cheeks. I couldn't explain the feeling. There wasn't a new revelation—the doctor gave no indication—I simply had a strong feeling deep in my gut.

The day after the biopsy, my stepdad was released from the hospital. The following week I couldn't shake what had come over me in the hospital. I shared with my children, son-in-law, and husband my urgency to get together with my stepdad. We needed to tell him we loved him because it could be our last opportunity to do so. The weekend of my mom's sixty-seventh birthday—to her surprise—we all showed up at their house. I couldn't have told you the last time we were all together.

My relationship with my mom unfortunately had not changed throughout the years. I visited her only when absolutely necessary. The negativity that flowed through her was suffocating. Everything I did or said was wrong, and I would have to hear about it for the entire visit. I didn't have to worry about her coming over to my house because she wouldn't choose to do so. The last time I recall her coming to my house was when we had allowed her to live in our basement for several months during a brief separation between her and my stepdad. That time was such a nightmare for me, I swore I would never allow her to stay again.

During this visit, we were sitting in the family room together when my stepdad started to cry. I believed he knew he was dying.

He focused on his grandchildren. "Don't do drugs. I did, and look at the mess I've made." His hand shook as he tapped his chest. "I did this to myself. Don't make the same mistakes—"

"You were always a screw up," Mom interrupted, and not for the last time.

The more he tried to be open and honest with his grandkids, the more Mom interrupted and tore him down. When I couldn't take the abuse Mom dished out to my stepdad, I headed to the back porch where I sat and cried. Why did she feel the need to tear him down?

My stepdad came outside and sat beside me. As we both cried, he put his arm around me and sighed.

"Sorry I made you cry."

I laid my head on his shoulder. "It's not you. I don't understand why she is so mean. I can handle her talking to me like that, but you? When you're so sick? Doesn't she know you're . . ." I couldn't bring myself to say the inevitable.

"When's your next day off?"

I worked two jobs fourteen to eighteen hours a day, six to seven days a week, so time off was a rarity, but his timing was perfect.

"I'm off tomorrow for Labor Day," I said.

"Want to go to lunch? Just the two of us?"

"I would love that."

Before we left, Charlie hugged each of us and told the kids and my husband how much he loved them. Even though the visit was a hard one, I'm so grateful we went because it was the last time my family saw him alive.

The following day I went to pick him up to go to lunch. I walked into an argument between my mother and stepdad over pain medicine.

"I need a pain pill," Charlie pleaded. He held on to the back of a chair, his body seemed to tremble from pain.

"There's nothing wrong with you. You just want to take one for no good reason," Mom yelled.

Between the day before and the current argument, something within me snapped, and I screamed loud enough to match my mom's volume. "Give him his medicine *now*. I didn't drive almost an hour to take Charlie out to eat and have him be miserable the entire time."

Mom glared at me. "He's not going to eat anyway; you're wasting your time."

I glared back. After realizing I wasn't backing down from the fight, my mom said to us, "Get out of the room so I can get the damn pill."

Charlie wasn't allowed to even see where she hid them.

We left after he took his medicine. Ten minutes into the drive my stepdad broke down. I have replayed this conversation in my mind a million times since he's been gone.

"Amy, I love your mom so much and would do anything I could for her."

I glanced at him and wondered why.

He wept as he continued. "I would never treat her like she's been treating me. I think I am dying. I feel so sick and weak and hurt so bad. Your mom is mad because I can't work. You see what I have to go through when I need a pain pill."

Seeing him cry ripped my heart out. I wanted to pull the car over and hug him. I wanted to make everything better. I hated what my mom did and how she made my stepdad feel. I hated that I couldn't do anything. We drove around for over an hour, talking and looking for a restaurant, but everywhere we went was closed for the holiday.

My stepdad said, "Let's just go back home."

"Not yet." I was determined to find an eating establishment and wasn't ready for our time alone together to be over.

After an hour and a half, we found a small family restaurant. Knowing my stepdad had consumed very little food over several weeks, I was happy to see him eat. On the ride home, he mentioned he struggled going up and down the stairs to bed.

"I'm afraid I'm going to fall," he said.

"Let me help move your bed into the spare room downstairs. There's plenty of room for your bed."

"Your mom will never allow you to do that."

I took a deep breath, then exhaled. "I'm not afraid of my mom. Not anymore. I'll be back Wednesday to move your bed."

Later when we returned home, I told my mom how much he'd eaten.

She huffed. "The only reason he ate anything was to prove me wrong. I know he didn't want to eat and that he was wasting your time by letting you take him. He wasted your time anyway. What took you so long to get back?"

"I stopped at the store and bought him some Ensures to drink when he doesn't feel like he can eat."

Mom huffed again.

I hugged my stepdad. "Bye. I'll see you in two days."

"Why?" Mom folded her arms.

I told her my plan to move his bed.

Anger built up in her face before her verbal attack. "You will not. Why are you giving in to him? He's just being a baby. He can walk up and down those steps just fine."

I narrowed my eyes and yelled back. "Just watch me. I will be moving it." I left before she could say anything else.

I never made it back to move his bed. Because I didn't have the opportunity to move him downstairs, I struggled with losing him for a very long time. Even though something told me the end was near, I wasn't mentally prepared for his death.

The day after I spent the afternoon with my stepdad, my daughter went into labor with her first child two weeks early. The same day I'd planned to move Charlie's bed, my grandson Luke was born. During labor, my daughter ran a fever. As a precaution, Luke was sent to the neonatal intensive care unit to get assessed for infection. Not long after he returned to the mother-baby unit, he had an apneic episode and stopped breathing for twenty-five seconds. We went from being ecstatic over his birth to panicking. Immediately he was sent back to the NICU for the next five days.

Four days after the birth of my grandson I'd left work at seven in the morning to sit with my daughter. Exhausted after being awake for twenty-seven hours, I had turned my phone off and didn't get my mom's call. I waited until I got in the car to listen to the voice mail she'd left me several hours earlier.

"Amy, you have to get over here and do something with Charlie, this is what I've had to listen to all day!" she screamed.

I assumed she'd held the phone toward something she wanted me to hear, but I didn't hear anything until she screamed again.

"He's been lying in bed all day moaning and hollering he's dying. I'm ready to knock the hell out of him; I can't take it anymore. I need you to get over here and do something. I'm not nurse material."

I gripped the steering wheel. Are you kidding me? How could someone be so cold? If I left right then and headed straight to her house, I wouldn't be there until 10:30 p.m. Beyond exhausted, I couldn't deal with my mom, and I figured my stepdad would be asleep before I arrived. I went home, deciding I'd call her in the morning and see if she still needed me to head over. The decision to go home has haunted me for several years.

My phone rang at 8:00 a.m.

"Amy, I can't wake him up!"

I bolted upright in bed. "What? What are you talking about, Mom?"

"He won't wake up. I'm trying to put his clothes on but he won't move. I don't know what to do."

"Did you call 911?"

"No, only thing I could think of was to call you."

Frantic and grabbing clothes, I screamed at her, "Call 911, I'm on my way!"

Having heard me scream, my husband entered our bedroom. I filled him in as I threw on my clothes and ran to the car. He called his mom and asked her to go to my mom's house until I arrived since my trip would take close to an hour.

Once on the road, I called my sister Lisa and told her about the phone call. She lived fifteen minutes away and could get there sooner. Halfway there I received another call. The woman on the other end was with the rescue squad.

"Mrs. Collier? How far away are you?"

I swallowed the lump in my throat. "Fifteen minutes." I increased my speed.

"Okay, we wanted to make sure you were close before we left. Your mom needs you right now."

Panic poured over me. As my voice shook, I asked, "Is my stepdad gone?"

"Yes. He's been gone for a while."

I hung up the phone, then screamed and cried. "This can't be happening! Why didn't I go last night? I should have gone. I should have been there."

When I arrived, my mom, Lisa, and my mother-in-law were sitting around the kitchen table talking. My mother-in-law hugged me.

"We're waiting on the coroner to pick up his body," she said.

I briefly looked in the direction of my mom.

"Hey Mimi," she said calling me by the nickname my sister's children called me. Mom acted as though it were a normal day.

I walked out of the room toward the upstairs. A police officer stood at the bottom of the steps. He tried to tell me I shouldn't go up there, but I kept walking. Outside my stepdad's bedroom door was another police officer.

"Miss, I don't think you should enter. It would be best if you didn't see him."

Nobody was going to stop me from seeing my stepdad and telling him how sorry I was for not being there. I pushed past him and opened the bedroom door.

I thought I'd walk into the room, and he would look like he was asleep. At least that's what I had prepared myself to see. I wasn't even close. For the life of me I will never understand how my mom didn't know he was dead when she tried to wake and dress him. Rigor mortis had already set in.

His eyes and mouth were opened with dried blood on his chin and lips. There was also dried blood on the side of his pillowcase and the fitted sheet. His hands and legs were contorted. There was a small trash can beside his bed where he had been vomiting—half full of blood and chunks of something that wasn't food. There was also a whole Valium. Mom later told me she had given him a Valium to help him go to sleep around midnight, then went to bed in her bedroom next to his and went to sleep.

I laid my head on his chest and cried. I told him how much I loved him and said over and over, "I'm sorry, I'm so sorry."

Through the vent in the floor, I heard my mom talking and laughing as though her husband weren't lying in the bed dead. I couldn't wrap my mind around any of what was taking place. He was gone. He had died in his room alone and in pain, and my mom talked and laughed downstairs as though nothing had happened.

Anger swelled inside of me. The sound of her voice made my skin crawl. I understand now that my mom was probably in shock and that everyone deals with death in a different way, but I wanted to run downstairs, bust into the kitchen, flip the furniture over, scream, curse, and cause her harm. I couldn't breathe. The guilt I felt for not going the night before overwhelmed me. I was devastated he'd died alone. My stepdad did not deserve to die like he did. How bad had he suffered?

My husband entered the room, held me, and talked me into going back downstairs. I went straight outside. I didn't want to look at my mom or hear her voice. I sat on the back-porch steps and tried to pull myself together. I made the dreaded phone calls to notify family and friends. Someone brought me mom's address book while I sat outside and asked me to call my stepdad's friends. My mom said she couldn't bring herself to do it.

She couldn't make phone calls? She had a hard time? Did she really think it was easy for me? From the way my mom had been laughing and talking, I struggled to see why she couldn't make calls. Why was everything always put on me? My whole life I'd been the one expected to take care of everyone, the one called when someone needed something or when something went wrong. My family expected me to figure it out and fix it.

The next several days passed by in a blur. I know I went to the funeral home to help make the arrangements. I planned the flowers, arranged a preacher, and my friend Jai purchased my stepdad's urn. With no life insurance, we all pitched in. I remember stressing over not having enough money to have a funeral. I bought food to take to my mom's house afterward, and I spent one night at her house with her so she wouldn't be alone. As I sat on the floor going through pictures of Charlie, Mom talked about how angry she was he'd left her. I forced myself to keep my mouth shut about how angry I was at her for how she had treated him.

The level of my emotions for months after Charlie's death was off the chart. Every time I closed my eyes, I saw him on his bed. I couldn't count the number of times I played the voice mail from my mom the night before he died. Each time I heard the message, I grew angrier toward my mom, along with the guilt and anger I felt toward myself for not going over there.

Several weeks after his passing I read the medical examiner's report. He hadn't died from cirrhosis of the liver as we all believed but from metastatic carcinoma. All his organs were so eaten up with cancer no one could identify which organ the cancer had started in. Although my stepdad had a biopsy done two weeks prior to his death after a mass had been found on his liver, he had passed away before we received the results.

The information helped ease some of the anger I carried toward my mother, knowing if she had called 911 the outcome would have been the same. He may have been more comfortable had she made the call, but the doctors couldn't have saved him.

CHAPTER 18

Roller-Coaster Ride from Hell

About a year after my stepdad, Charlie, passed away, my mom lost everything. Her car was repossessed and her home foreclosed. At the time of my stepdad's death, his income was all they had. My mom had not worked in years. Due to his illness, he hadn't worked for several weeks prior. They were already behind on bills. It took several months before my mom started collecting a social security check. By then, she was in a hole she never could get out of.

I occasionally received a phone call asking if I could pay an electric bill but only after her electricity had already been turned off and not beforehand when I could have prevented it and avoided a reconnect fee. Maybe it was humiliating for her to ask, like admitting she couldn't take care of herself. Coming up with the money to pay bills was foreign to her—she never needed to in the past.

Depression set in, and Mom stayed awake all night and slept all day. She rarely bathed, and unopened mail piled up. I felt it was her way of shutting everyone and everything out. Mom became unavailable to the world. She slept during business hours so making phone calls to take care of things was impossible. Because she got out of bed as everyone else prepared for sleep, she didn't have to see or talk to anyone, including her family.

After losing her home, I helped Mom move in with my little sister. They still had a strained relationship, but Mom didn't have any place to go, and, deep down, my sister wanted to have a relationship with her and wanted her children to have one with their grandma.

Unfortunately, after a year, the relationship ended badly, and I found myself once again moving Mom's stuff. This time she moved closer to live with my oldest sister in a nearby town. Around a year and a half later that also ended when Lisa moved out of the state.

I felt like the three of us girls had all tried in our own ways to have a relationship with our mom, but to no avail for one reason or another. It was easier for me to avoid her than to listen to her negativity about anything and everything I said. I dreaded her end-of-the-month phone call when she needed me to get her something from the store because she was out of money until she received her next social security check. Sometimes I would see her for a few minutes when I dropped off whatever she needed, but most of the time she would be asleep when I got there, so I left the purchases on the door or table.

I knew a long time ago that for me to move forward and heal, and also for my own sanity, I had to distance myself from my mom. My heart broke every time I said that, but it was the reality of my relationship with her.

In August 2017, I called my mom several days before her birthday to tell her I would take time off from work on September 1 and pick her up to go shopping for some new clothes. With the approach of winter, I knew she didn't have anything warm enough that wasn't falling off her. She'd lost a lot of weight since my stepdad passed. I was not surprised when she called the night before her birthday and said she wasn't coming. She claimed she wasn't feeling well. Deep down I never expected her to go and was waiting on her excuse to back out. I told her I didn't know when I would have another day available to take her, but she was adamant about not going.

Sunday morning, two days after Mom's birthday, Charlie and I decided to go for a long drive. We'd had a huge argument and a very tough week of not getting along, so we wanted to spend some time together. Twenty minutes into our drive, we stopped to get gas. When Charlie got out of the car, my cell phone rang, and Mom's name appeared on the caller ID. I hit the silent button. Soon, my phone's notification told me I had a voice mail. I assumed she would ask me to take her to the grocery store since it was the third of the month, and it was the day her social security check would be credited to her bank account. At first, I wasn't going to listen to the message right away but would listen to it when we returned home. Something told me not to wait. I looked at Charlie pumping gas, then played the message.

"Amy, I just woke up. I've been asleep since I hung up the phone with you the other day. I need you to go to Walmart and get my insulin. I've been out for two weeks. I also either fell or fainted going to the bathroom. I don't know which. Could you please go get my medicine?"

Could her timing have been any worse? I knew Charlie would flip out if I had to go back for my mom. There was no way I would tell him, not after the week we'd had, so I planned to go to the store when we got back home. The message replayed in my mind. My gut told me she needed to go to the doctor, but my head screamed Charlie would be furious if I told him to take me back home.

When Charlie got back inside the car and was pulling out of the parking lot, I blurted, "I have to go back home; my mom called." I explained the voice mail.

The angry glare he sent my way and his choice of words made his fury clear. I regretted telling him about Mom's phone call and wished I'd gone on our road trip. That is until I found out the severity of her condition.

I returned her call. "I'll be there in fifteen minutes. Be ready. I'm taking you to urgent care."

Like usual, she screamed back at me. "I'm not going anywhere. Just get my medicine like I asked you too. I just need my medicine."

I gritted my teeth. "Yes, you are. If you've been sleeping for two days, you're going to the doctor if I have to put you in the car myself."

After she'd ruined my time with Charlie and I had to deal with his anger, I wasn't about to give in to her. To my surprise, when I got to her house she was dressed and ready to go. I still had to hear her complaints about how unnecessary it was to go to urgent care, but at least I didn't need to physically put her in my car. The closest urgent care was twenty minutes away. Halfway to the doctor's office, Mom spoke up.

"Oh, I forgot to tell you, around four in the morning on Friday I woke up and had a very bad pain in the side of my neck. It ran down my shoulder and arm to my elbow. I was going to call you but saw it was 4:00 a.m., so I just went back to bed. It hurt really bad. Do you think I had a heart attack?"

I looked over at her. "You're freaking kidding me right now. You just now thought to tell me this, two days later?"

"Well, I've been asleep since it happened," she replied.

I seriously didn't understand this woman. When we arrived, I told the receptionist about Mom being asleep for two days and the pain she had experienced prior.

She was taken to the back where they checked her blood sugar and did an EKG. Her blood sugar was extremely high, which was no surprise since she had been without insulin for two weeks, and the EKG was abnormal.

"Why did you wait so long to come in?" the doctor questioned my mom.

"Wouldn't be here today if my daughter hadn't made me come." She cut her eyes at me.

I doubted Mom understood the severity of the situation.

"She needs to go to the hospital, now," the doctor told both of us.

From the look on my mom's face, I knew what was coming next.

"Just give me my medicine and let me go home! I don't need to go anywhere in an ambulance." She spewed a string of curse words.

I told Mom she would either go to hospital by ambulance or I was taking her in my car, but either way she was going. When she realized I was not backing down, she agreed to go. Mom spewed more of her anger toward the ambulance drivers.

The doctor who'd seen my mom, approached me and said, "God love you."

At least someone seemed to understand what my mom put me through.

At the hospital, Mom's rude behavior continued. I was mortified. She argued with both the doctor and nurse over every test they wanted to run. Eventually, I picked up the book I'd brought with me to try to block her out by reading.

With another string of profanity, she yelled for me to put my book down.

I calmly looked at her. "It is in your best interest to let me read." Then I continued to do so. With the level of anger rising in me I knew I could say something I would regret, and the hospital was not the time nor the place to speak my mind. I needed a distraction, and reading was the only tool I had with me.

After looking at all the test results, the doctor wanted to admit my mom.

"Mrs. Overstreet, you're either having a heart attack or recently had one. The only way to know for sure is to monitor your blood work during the night."

Mom refused. "I don't need any more tests. It's my sugar, not my heart. Give me my medicine and let me go home."

"It's actually both." The doctor looked at her chart. "And your kidney function is very low. You really need to stay."

My mom folded her arms and glared at me. "Amy, take me home. Now."

I lost it. "You have totally lost your mind if you think I am taking you home. All I can say is you better start walking, and it's a forty-five-minute drive by car."

She stared at me as if to say, how dare you to talk to me like that. She raised her chin in defiance. "The ambulance brought me here; they can take me home."

"Mom, the ambulance is not a taxi service. That's not how it works." I pointed toward the door. "Start walking."

She turned to the doctor. "I guess I'm staying. Apparently, I don't have a choice."

I got up and went outside to smoke a cigarette before I choked her. I texted my siblings and husband to let them know what was going on, then went back in to sit with my mom until bedtime. Exhausted, I headed home. The following morning when

I returned to the hospital, the doctor told me that the troponin level in Mom's blood had been very high upon her arrival. As the night passed, it lowered, which indicated Mom had had a heart attack two days before when she experienced pain in the side of her neck that traveled down to her elbow. However, in the early morning hours the troponin level rose again, which indicated she was having another heart attack. The doctor scheduled an emergency catheterization.

During Mom's procedure I sat alone in the waiting room and tried to wrap my head around the events of the past twenty-four hours. Right before the doctor came out, my husband walked into the waiting room. I was surprised to see him there but also very grateful not to be alone. The doctor led us to a private room to discuss his findings.

"Forty-five percent of your mom's heart is dead and no longer functioning due to the heart attack. Of the remaining 55 percent, we need to perform six bypasses and a valve repair." He paused as if waiting for me to absorb the information. "There's a very high chance your mother won't survive the surgery. Her kidney function is very low, and we're having difficulty getting her blood sugar level under control. It would be ideal if we could wait to do the surgery until everything else has stabilized, but with her having had two massive heart attacks in three days, I don't believe we have a choice. Without having the surgery as soon as possible, she will not survive."

I buried my face in my husband's chest and sobbed. *I don't want her to die*, was all I could think about. We returned to the waiting room to give me time to calm down. I looked at Charlie.

"Why am I crying? It's not like we had a relationship."

"She's still your mom, Amy," he replied.

After she was settled in the intensive care unit, I went outside to call my sisters to let them know what the doctor had said. I didn't want Mom to hear me. I struggled to keep my emotions together but failed.

The doctor explained to Mom and me what the surgery would entail and the high chance of not surviving. Mom agreed to have the open-heart surgery, which was scheduled for 6:30 the following morning. As the day turned into night, my fear of losing my mom turned into panic. I thought about her soul and how she wasn't saved. I headed to the waiting area and called my youngest son, Charles. I cried hysterically, asking him to please come to the hospital as soon as possible. Because of my sobs it took him a few minutes to understand what I was saying, then he reassured me he was on his way. Charles was nineteen years old and an ordained minister. I wanted him to pray over Mom and for her surgery. In my fear and panic I knew I needed him with me too. To this day I'm so grateful he came.

Mom's face lit up when he walked into the room. He carried with him a sense of peace and calmness. After visiting with his grandmother for a few minutes, he asked her if she had ever asked Jesus for forgiveness for all her sins and if she would like to say a prayer with him. Any other time my mom would have gotten defensive and that would have been the end of the conversation, but this time—to my amazement—she looked him straight in his eyes and said yes.

My older sister and her husband had arrived at the hospital soon after I'd called Charles. With the five of us in the room, we bowed our heads as Charles and my mom prayed. The panic I'd been feeling was soon gone and replaced with peace. I could also see peace across Mom's face as well. Regardless of what was to happen the following morning, my mom was saved.

Before Mom headed to surgery, I, my older sister, her husband, my little sister, and her son all gave Mom a hug and a kiss and told her we loved her. I was so proud of my little sister for being there. Their relationship had been estranged for several years, and to see them put their differences aside and express their love for each other made my heart happy. I was also grateful not to be at the hospital alone during the six-hour open heart surgery where the odds were against my mom.

Surprisingly, since Mom had been admitted to the hospital, she had been cooperative, which was a little unnerving considering I knew how she could be. She never showed fear or shed a single tear. She even laughed at me once when I was sitting beside her with tears running down my face.

"You worry too much," she said.

Mom never showed the emotions you would normally expect at the proper time. She didn't cry—at least rarely—and she didn't show love or affection. Sadly, at times, I wondered how she could be human with such a lack of any emotion other than anger.

Mom survived her surgery and was taken off the ventilator later that night. My oldest sister left to return home and said she would be back in a couple of weeks. The doctors told us she could go home in a couple of days, so my little sister and I agreed on how we would take care of Mom. Puddy would stay during the day while I worked, then I would stay with Mom after work until her bedtime.

The bad time seemed to have passed, but we were about to embark on a roller-coaster ride straight from hell.

CHAPTER 19

The Unwanted Caregiver

The following day while at work I received a hysterical phone call from my little sister.

"Get here now! The doctors couldn't regulate Mom's heart rate. Amy, they stopped her heart on purpose! The doctor said he needed to restart her heart to regulate it. She's got a lot of fluid draining. They can't take out her chest tubes." She sobbed. "Mom's kidney functions are still very low; her blood sugar is out of control. I can't do this by myself, I just can't."

Two days later Mom was placed back on the ventilator. A lot of fluid remained around her lungs, and the doctors were concerned it would turn into pneumonia. They also had to put her on a temporary pacemaker due to her heart going into atrial fibrillation (A-fib) and because the medication was not working. My new morning ritual became this: wake at 5:30 a.m., call the hospital, get a report of the events during the night. The information I'd receive would determine if I was able to go to work or needed to go straight to the hospital. Afterward I'd send a mass text to my siblings and family. Her stability during the day determined how late I'd stay at night.

For six days I sat in silence and watched the ventilator breathe for Mom while she was sedated and not aware of anything. Mom had two different IVs happening at the same time. At one point, her right arm swelled up and turned a dark purple. Several times her arm became so swollen her skin tore. The IVs were moved to her left arm and the left side of her neck.

The nurses were awesome and kept me informed of every step forward Mom made and every step backward. Besides battling with her heart, kidney, and sugar issues, she now had to deal with scar tissue damage to her lungs. She was soon diagnosed with chronic obstructive pulmonary disease (COPD).

Four days after she was taken off the ventilator, Mom was moved from the ICU into the step-down unit on the third floor. They left the feeding tube in but allowed her to have puréed food. Mom wouldn't eat or cooperate with nurses. Her speech was unintelligible, and she began to hallucinate. Once again, the temporary pacemaker was turned on due to the A-fib, and my mom was treated for a urinary tract infection. The following day I received a phone call saying they were going to do a blood transfusion. Mom had lost a unit of blood, and the doctors didn't know from where or why. The next day she received two more units of blood, and by day three Mom was headed back to intensive care.

A couple hours after my sister called me at work to tell me they were moving Mom back to the ICU, she called me back crying. I was already on my way to the hospital.

"The doctor wants to put Mom back on the ventilator. I told them they couldn't until they talked to you. Don't let them do it, Amy. Mom can't take anymore," she pleaded.

When I walked into the intensive care unit, the doctor was waiting for me at the nurses' station.

"Your mother's lungs are full of fluid again. I suspect the pneumonia has returned." He held my gaze. "I can assure you if I thought we were at a point of no longer being able to help her, I would tell you. However, we're not at that point yet."

"What'll happen if we don't put her back on the ventilator?" I asked.

He sighed. "We would make her as comfortable as possible by sedating her, but she would suffocate."

I shook my head. "No, I can't do that. My little sister doesn't want our mom back on the ventilator, but Lisa needs to be in on the decision."

Puddy, the doctor, and I stood around Mom's bed as I called Lisa and explained everything while having her on speakerphone.

"Puddy doesn't want to, but I think we should let the doctor ventilate Mom," I said.

After a long pause, Lisa spoke up. "I agree with Puddy. Amy, she's gone through enough."

"Why quit now when you've come this far?" The doctor didn't mask the frustration in his voice. "Give her twenty-four hours. If you're still against it, we'll turn off the ventilator."

After several minutes of back and forth, Lisa agreed to the twenty-four hours. To be completely honest, I would have made sure Mom was put back on the ventilator no matter whether Lisa changed her mind. I wouldn't have been able to live with myself otherwise. I wanted Lisa's opinion, but it would never have been the deciding factor.

When I hung up the phone, Puddy glared at me then stormed out of the room.

I didn't try to stop my tears when a nurse approached and held my hand.

"I don't know what the right thing is to do. I just know I can't let her die this way," I said. I spoke into Mom's ear. "Mom, please tell me what you want. Do you want them to put you back on the ventilator?" She nodded even though neither sister was present to see it. "Okay, they're bringing in the stuff now. I'm going to get out of the way, but I'll be back."

I left Mom's room and went looking for my sister. I found her crying in the chapel. I sat beside her.

She turned toward me. "Amy, why do you have to be so selfish? Why are you playing God?"

I held her hand. "I'm not. If God is ready to take Mom, He will take her. It doesn't matter if she is on a ventilator or not."

We talked for a while, and she calmed down. It had been fifteen days since Mom's surgery, and we were both dealing with stress levels with nonstop highs and lows, never knowing what to expect from hour to hour.

As we walked back into her room, Mom was gagging.

Puddy faced me. "You think this is what is best for Mom?" she screamed. "I'm not coming back as long as Mom's on a ventilator!" She left the room cursing as she went down the hall. True to her words, she never came back.

Almost instantly, Mom calmed.

"I'm so sorry," the nurse said. "I needed to get the correct amount of medication she needed. We want her to be comfortable but not completely sedated. She still needs to be able to respond."

Within a half hour, Mom seemed to relax.

"Feeling better?" I asked.

She nodded.

Mom was on the ventilator for five days. Over three of those days she received three more units of blood. Her heart went in and out of A-fib several times. Her blood pressure medication needed to be adjusted, and the nurses needed to remove an abundance of mucus from the back of her throat. On the fourth day her sedation medication was increased and her left hand tied down because she kept trying to pull out the feeding tube. Mom fought to take out her feeding tube because, after having it in for twenty days, she complained her throat hurt.

There was no need to restrain her right arm because she hadn't been able to lift it since the veins were blown several weeks prior. It was still swollen and badly bruised. Nobody was allowed to touch her right arm.

When Mom was finally taken off the ventilator, she struggled to breathe, which caused her to be placed onto a BiPAP machine. A BiPAP machine is a type of ventilator that pushes pressurized air into your lungs and helps open the lungs with air pressure. Instead of the tube down Mom's throat into her lungs, she wore a mask connected to the ventilator.

The battle to breathe continued, and, for the second time since the drainage tubes had been removed after Mom's surgery, the doctor had to put a chest tube back in on the right side due to excess fluid around her lung. Mom wore the BiPAP during the night to give her lungs a rest and had breathing treatments every three to four hours after coming off the ventilator. On top of everything else, Mom pulled her feeding tube out for the second time, and, since she failed the swallow test, they had to put it back in.

I was beyond emotionally drained, and my stress level was off the charts. Every step Mom took forward, she seemed to take multiple steps back, which repeated from hour to hour for almost a month. Night after night (and many days) I sat by myself with my mom, much of the time in silence. Mom was either asleep or sedated depending on the events of the day. My world was dictated by my mom's good days and bad ones. Her ups and downs determined whether I could go to work, see my husband, my kids, or my grandkids for brief snippets of time. Some weeks I didn't see my family at all. Because of my time at the hospital, the staff knew my first name, and the night shift in the cafeteria had my coffee ready and would ring it up before I got to the cash register. Most days, the hospital workers were the only communication I had with another person besides talking to Mom, who wasn't conscious during a lot of our conversations. I felt isolated from the world.

I spent hours over multiple nights brushing the matted knots out of the back of Mom's head from where she hadn't been able to sit up for the past month. Every once in a while, she would wake up and yell at me to stop, then turn her head. I would move to the other side of the bed and start working on that side of her head until she would wake up and yell at me again. She'd turn her head again, and I would go back to where I'd started the process.

One evening my husband stopped in to see us, and when he was ready to leave, Mom told him she loved him. I noticed, on the rare occasion she had a visitor, Mom always told them she loved them when they left. But every night when I told Mom I loved her, she wouldn't say it back.

When Charlie walked out of the room, I looked at her. "You know, that's really screwed up."

She raised her brow. "What?"

"You have told every single person who has stopped by that you love them. I've been here every single day since you've been in this hospital, and I tell you I love you. You don't say a word. That's really screwed up, Mom."

She looked at me, surprised. "Well, you already know."

I crossed my arms. "Seriously, Mom? No, I don't."

After that night, before Mom went to sleep, she told me she loved me. I stayed at the hospital until she had her breathing treatment and was put on the BiPAP for the night. Once she fell asleep, I would leave. Because I lived forty-five minutes away from the hospital, I arrived home between eleven and midnight, well past everyone's bedtime.

On day thirty at Lynchburg General Hospital—a short-term hospital—Mom had overstayed her time limit and needed to be transported to Virginia Baptist Hospital, a long-term hospital where she would remain until she was ready to go to a rehabilitation center. Mom's health issues continued. Her blood pressure remained too low, fluid in her lungs necessitated a chest tube, nourishment was still through a feeding tube, and at night she needed the BiPAP.

The roller-coaster ride from hell continued. I wouldn't let myself get excited whenever she made progress because I knew all too well how things could change within the hour and usually did. Even after her transfer, I remained mentally and physically exhausted. My normal workday consisted of cleaning houses, which left me alone with my thoughts, not always a good thing. Being at the hospital meant watching Mom sleep 99 percent of the time. The routine continued when I returned home at night and everyone was already in bed. I felt more and more isolated as the days went by.

Less than a week after Mom was moved to Virginia Baptist Hospital, she had a chest X-ray, which showed her chest tube had a kink in it, and fluid was building up around her lung. She was sent back to Lynchburg General Hospital to have the tube replaced with a new one.

I received a phone call saying mom was once again in the ICU. When I arrived at the hospital, I wasn't prepared for what had happened. As the nurses removed the chest tube, Mom had started throwing up blood. Within minutes she had gone into respiratory arrest and coded.

The next four days consisted of taking tubes out, putting tubes back in, putting Mom on the BiPAP, taking her off the BiPAP, then repeat. An infection had developed around the site of her chest tube, and she had a urinary tract infection.

Mom was confused and hallucinating. She asked me if I saw the puppy in the hall. I looked in the hall and said no. She looked at me as though I'd lost my mind.

"You need glasses, Amy. It's right there by the door."

The day before she was transported back to Virginia Baptist Hospital, I walked in her room, and she had dried blood around her nose and a hook inside of her nose and around the feeding tube. Anger rose in me.

"Mom, what's going on."

"Amy, they hurt me." Defeat filled her words.

I stormed out of her room and headed for the nurses' station. The nurse told me Mom had pulled the feeding tube out again, which was about the fifth time in five weeks. Having watched the process of a feeding tube being inserted, I had no idea why my mom continued to put herself in a position to have it reinserted. I believed the urinary tract infection played a part in her removing the tube the last time because of the mental state of confusion she was in. I was still upset with the solution of keeping the tube in.

Mom was transported back to Virginia Baptist Hospital on October 11, back to Lynchburg General on the twelfth to have fluid pulled off her lung, then returned to Baptist in the evening. Every transport exhausted my mom to the point she'd sleep for the next day or two. She began to have low blood pressure again, and her heart kept going in and out of A-fib. On the sixteenth she was transported back to Lynchburg General to have a chest tube put back in only to return again three days later to have it removed and relocated because it had not been placed in the correct spot. Mom's oxygen levels rapidly dropped. I asked the doctor why we were still having so many issues with her breathing. For the first time I was informed Mom's lung had collapsed when she was taken off the ventilator a month prior and had not returned to proper function.

Why had no one told me before now? Would I ever wake up from this never-ending nightmare?

After seven weeks in the hospital, Mom was put on a full liquid diet, but the feeding tube remained in place. A week later she was promoted to a puréed diet. Again. Swallowing was a major struggle for her. The nurse or I would spray her throat to numb it a few minutes before she tried to eat. She complained about her throat hurting and said it felt like she was swallowing glass. Mom had lost her voice and could barely whisper. I complained daily about wanting the feeding tube taken out.

The medical team said she wasn't eating enough, but she couldn't eat because of still being fed through the feeding tube. Swallowing with the tube down her raw throat was a challenge. Mom was fighting a losing battle. The doctor agreed to turn the feeding tube off during the day but would turn it back on from 6:00 p.m. to 6:00 a.m.

Two days later Mom received a unit of blood, but the doctor still could not find where she was losing blood. Later, I found out the loss of blood was from her throat. I'd had enough. I called Mom's palliative care team who had become involved when Mom had gone into respiratory arrest three weeks prior. I explained to them my concerns with the feeding tube and how it had been in my mom's throat for nine weeks.

"It's not recommended for a patient to have one for longer than two weeks," the care team member said. "Tell your mother's nurse you want to put in an order to remove it and to have the palliative care team back in to see her."

The meeting was to take place in two days

I got to the hospital a few minutes before the scheduled meeting, and to my surprise Mom's feeding tube had been removed. I was told the day before it was not going to be removed until Mom was eating 1,500 calories a day. With the tube gone, the change in Mom's spirits was apparent.

The palliative care team member was also surprised. "Glad the feeding tube was removed. Sometimes it takes calling someone in to monitor the situation to get this done in a timely manner." She nodded. "I'll be back in a couple of days to see how things are going. If your mother is still struggling to eat, ask the doctor to put her on medication to increase her appetite."

The nurses taped a piece of paper to Mom's door and wrote down everything she ate and the amount.

Around 1:00 a.m. the following morning the hospital called. When the nurse had gone to check on Mom, she could open her eyes but couldn't move or speak. Her blood sugar level had dropped to thirty-seven. The nurse said at 8:00 p.m. the previous night her level had been at two hundred fifty-seven, so she'd received insulin.

Based on the drop in Mom's sugar levels, the doctor decided Mom was not to receive insulin at night. When I got to the hospital later in the morning, Mom was shaken up but felt better.

I asked her, "How many lives do you have? I swear you're like a cat. I am convinced you're trying to kill me."

She laughed. "I'm not going anywhere."

"I see that," I replied.

Mom was like a different person that day. She was so happy when her brother Jimmy from Delaware came to see her. Her face lit up whenever she talked about him. His visit was a much needed one. Finally, we had a good day.

After a total of sixty-six days, Mom was released from the hospital and transported to rehab to learn to walk again. I never thought the day would arrive for the roller-coaster ride to end.

CHAPTER 20

The Final Chapter

I thought the nightmare we experienced had ended and we were headed for a time to heal and recover. I was mistaken. We continued into the same roller-coaster ride of emotions, stress, and heartbreak when Mom entered rehab. I sent Mom to the rehabilitation center where my daughter worked as a therapist. I knew Cindy would keep an eye on her. Up to that point, my daughter didn't have a relationship with her grandmother. She had only known her as her mom's mom. It never crossed my mind they would build a relationship and become as close as they did. I am forever grateful for that blessing.

I'd hoped the stress of running back and forth to the hospital would be over so Mom could rest and grow stronger. Unfortunately, that didn't happen either. The daily unknowns continued as it had the previous two months. Three different times 911 was called to transport Mom to the hospital. Once she fell out of bed, and the facility wanted to make sure nothing was broken. The second time she passed out and was unresponsive when the nurse tried to help her to the bathroom. That time, my daughter rode with her grandmother in the ambulance to the hospital. Mom's blood sugar had dropped to forty. Her temperature had also dropped, and as a result, she was suffering from hypothermia.

I was an hour and a half away at work and left for the hospital, fearing the worst. My heart pounded and my hands shook as I drove as fast as I could, trying to stay safe and see through my tears. My daughter texted me updates with what she knew. By the time I got to the hospital, Mom was stable. I walked into her room, and she looked at me.

"I'm back." She chuckled.

"This isn't funny, Mom," I snapped.

"I don't know why you and Cindy are so worried. You can't kill German blood. We're too tough," she said.

Making jokes was her way of dealing with every scary event happening to her. I never understood her humor.

Honestly, I felt like her health complications were secretly trying to kill me. How much more of this roller-coaster ride of emotions could my heart take? Every time my phone rang, I held my breath. I would hesitate before looking at the caller ID.

Mom tried as hard as she could in therapy but because of her congestive heart failure and COPD, she struggled to breathe and was put back on oxygen. The nurses continued to inform me when Mom's medication was increased due to fluid building up around her lungs. The third time the ambulance was called, Mom couldn't breathe. She was diagnosed with pneumonia for the second time since she'd been in the rehabilitation center.

Two weeks later I received another phone call from Mom's doctor. Even with my daughter calling first to warn me about the conversation, I wasn't ready to make one of the biggest decisions of my life.

"I'm sorry, Mrs. Collier, but your mother is no longer a candidate to stay at the rehabilitation center," the doctor said. "After an evaluation meeting with her nurse and therapist, I'm afraid it's time to call hospice."

The last bout with pneumonia had weakened Mom's heart, leaving her with only 30 percent functioning capability. Fluid continued to build around her lungs. She would not be able to improve with any further therapies. A decision had to be made to either move Mom to a nursing home or bring her home with me. After my phone conversation with the doctor, I had no idea how I'd tell Mom she was terminal. How do you tell someone they're dying? Should I put her in a nursing home to die surrounded by strangers? Or bring her home with me? How could I take care of her and work? Was I even capable? These questions and so many more jabbed at my thoughts.

Later, I went to see Mom like I'd done every day for four months. The first thirty minutes was our normal evening routine except for me trying hard to talk around the lump in my throat and holding back the tears knowing I had to have "the talk." Where were my siblings? Why did I have to do this alone? It was the single hardest talk of my life.

My mom didn't want to hear any of it. She didn't believe me.

"Stop lying to me, Amy. I'm getting better; I know I am. I'm not dying. I'll show those doctors."

Even though my mom didn't believe she was terminal, the thought of being placed in a nursing home terrified her. I struggled with my decision to bring her home. I wanted to do what was best for my mom, but why should I take care of the woman who was never a mom to me? But what kind of person would I be if I turned my back on her? Could I really live with myself if I put her in a nursing home to die? It didn't matter what she would have done had the roles been reversed. What mattered was what I would do. I wasn't my mom. Even if I'd wanted to walk away I never could or would. All I ever wanted was for Mom to want to be in my life and to have a relationship with me, but not like this.

For the last five months I'd been on this roller-coaster ride with her and—no matter what—I wasn't going to jump off now.

A decision was made. Mom would come home with me and my family. In the event things didn't work out, the nursing home would be the only other option.

I had two weeks to get ready for Mom's arrival. I cleared out our spare bedroom, which had been the grandkid's playroom. We painted the walls and purchased an adjustable bed since she couldn't breathe lying flat. We mounted a TV and installed cable. Hospice had delivered all the equipment she needed. Mom was transported by a nonemergency ambulance to our home since she couldn't walk. I had no way of getting her inside the house without help. The EMTs brought her in on a stretcher and got her into her bed.

My little sister put aside her differences and hurts our mother had caused her to help me care for Mom. Puddy came to the house in the mornings to care for Mom all day while I continued to work. She was my saving grace. She stayed until I returned home, fed the farm animals, and settled in. Without her help along with the hospice staff, I don't know what I would have done. I was aware life would be tough before I took Mom in, but I wasn't mentally prepared for the toll it took on all of us—me, my husband, children, grandchildren, and my marriage.

Taking care of my mom was the hardest thing I'd ever done in my entire life. She made it harder than it should have been or needed to be. More often I walked out of her bedroom and went outside to cry. After caring for my mom, I have nothing but admiration for caregivers; it's a sacrificial act and at times can be unappreciated and tiring. I was emotionally and physically exhausted. Since the beginning of her illness, my life had ceased to exist as my own, and every second of every day had revolved around her.

I was convinced my mom would hurt me until she took her last breath. Which was exactly what she tried to do.

I learned a lot during the last eight months of her life. One of the most important things was forgiveness is not always earned, but it's freely given. I chose to forgive her many times for many different reasons, more so for my mental health than for hers. I never knew three months could seem like an eternity and not long enough all at the same time. Saying my mom made taking care of her harder than it needed to be was an understatement. She made living with us a complete nightmare. I questioned the decision I made many times. I wanted to quit and, on several occasions, called the hospice nurse crying and told her I couldn't take care of my mom any longer. I wanted to give up. My life was on hold because I decided to take care of a dying woman who didn't want me to take care of her. Mom's nurse listened to me with understanding and let me cry until I mustered up enough strength to go back inside the house and try again.

Side by side with my mom, I witnessed her battling through her own anger, rage, depression, and confusion. Somehow everything became my fault. Often, she screamed, cursed, slapped me, or threw objects at me from across the room. Other times she sat in silence and stared at the wall, refusing to acknowledge my presence. We had moments when we laughed, cried, and argued. I never knew what each day would bring, and some days I received all the above on the same day. Too many nights I woke to the TV blaring from my mom's room. I either woke startled by the noise or slept through it from exhaustion. Charlie would wake me, yelling for me to get up and do something. Either way I jumped out of bed and ran to her bedroom. Nine times out of ten she had turned the volume up on the remote as loud as it would go, and then she'd thrown the remote control across the room. After several minutes of searching, I would snap at her.

"What are you doing? Go to sleep. I have to get up early to go to work!"

Mom always had an excuse for why she'd turned up the volume. Even with her excuses, deep down I believed it was on purpose. Since my stepdad's passing, Mom would stay up all night and sleep all day. As hard as we tried to get her back on a somewhat normal sleep schedule, nothing worked, making the nights the most challenging and stressful times. If she wasn't turning up the volume on the TV, she was trying to get out of bed, even though she knew she couldn't walk on her own and would fall and hurt herself. She threw things on the floor just because she could. There were days on my way home from work I would catch myself unconsciously taking the long way home because deep down I dreaded what was to come once I got there.

Two weeks later we had another long night with the TV. By then, we all seemed to be able to sleep as much as we could through the noise, and I refused to get up. In the morning when I went in to check on her before I left for work, I found things scattered everywhere. She'd pushed her breathing machine to the floor as well as everything on top of her night table and the hospital table beside the bed. I threw my hands up and stormed out.

When I returned home from work, Puddy met me.

"I asked Mom why she trashed her room," she said.

"And?" I folded my arms.

"She said since she'd stopped getting you up at night over the TV, she thought it was funny to destroy her room because she knew it would make you mad. She also said you deserved it."

I didn't think I could be angrier; I was wrong.

That evening as we did our routine of checking her blood sugar before dinner, deciding if she needed insulin followed by a shot then supper, we spoke very little. She knew I was still upset with her. After she ate, I sat at the end of her bed.

"We need to talk," I said.

Mom faced the wall.

"No matter what I do, it isn't good enough. I've never met anyone as mean as you."

She turned and glared at me. "Look in the mirror."

I shook my head. "Mom, I could look in the mirror all day every day and never see you staring back at me. I put my life on hold, knowing without a doubt you would never have done it for me if the roles were reversed. I brought you to my home so you wouldn't die alone in a nursing home, and you intentionally do things to cause added stress *and* cause Charlie to get mad at me. For whatever reason, you're doing your best to keep everyone up all night. Do you have any idea how disrespectful you're being? I have to go to work, Charlie has to get up early and go to work, and your grandson in the other room has to get up early to go to school. Have you even thought about how these are the memories you're leaving for him? He has no memories of you throughout his childhood. Is this how you want him to remember you? I can't do this any longer. You've left me no other choice but to make arrangements for you to go into a nursing home."

Mom turned away from me, and, after several minutes of sitting in silence, I left her room. Once again for the thousandth time I went outside, sat on the porch steps, sobbed, and prayed. Before I could make any arrangements, Mom's health declined rapidly as the reality of terminal illness sunk in. In my head I knew my mom was dying, but, in my heart, I never believed she was going to die. Once when the hospice nurse and I were talking about how many lives my mom had, I made the comment, "Satan doesn't die."

Mom developed pneumonia for the third time. Her health issues of suffering with COPD, congestive heart failure, diabetes, and anxiety took their toll. Even though she said she felt better, there would be no bouncing back from the damage to her lungs and heart. She went to sleep one day and slept for three. The hospice nurse told us she was unresponsive and not to expect her to regain consciousness, yet the third morning she woke up and wanted to talk to everyone, which she did. She held a cup and drank, something she hadn't been able to do in several weeks without spilling. She was hungry and actually ate. When the nurse arrived, she was surprised to see Mom responsive because her pulse and blood pressure were very low, her organs were shutting down, and the back side of her arms and legs had turned purple. Her body no longer responded to her insulin shots.

Aware of what was happening, my sister and I cried all day. Mom gave her wedding rings to the nurse who'd come to bathe her with these instructions: "Give these to Amy. I want her to have them," then asked her to put them in my hands.

I took the rings back to my mom's bedroom and put them back on her finger. "I don't want these now, but I know you want me to have them. I'll get them when you're gone."

I called the hospice nurse when Mom had hiccups for two days on top of her other issues.

"It could be because of the weakening of the heart muscle or inflammation around the heart. Is also can occur as a person nears death." The nurse's words were gentle, but hard to hear. "Go ahead and give her a low dose of morphine. It'll help her be comfortable."

No surprise, Mom argued. "I'm not taking morphine, *and* I'm not dying. I'm getting better. You'll see."

When she finally did agree to take the morphine, I put the medication in a dropper and handed it to Puddy to give Mom. A few seconds after my sister squirted the medicine into her mouth, Mom spit some on my sister then turned her head and spit the rest toward me. I screamed at her, and she just laughed. When I called the nurse and told her about the incident, she came and informed Mom she could either swallow the morphine or receive a shot.

After such a long day, I decided to take a bath. While the tub filled, I went to see if Mom needed anything.

"Why's this happening to me?"

I assumed she meant dying, not the ordeal with the morphine. "Mom, every time you've had pneumonia your lungs and heart have gotten weaker. They're too weak to keep working now."

I turned to leave when she spoke up. "Amy, I want you to go with me."

I looked back at her, confused. "Go with you where?"

With a serious look and in a matter-of-fact tone, she said, "You know."

I raised my brow. She wanted me to *die* with her? I responded, "How about you go, and I'll follow you." I got the mom look that moms give when you know you're about to get in trouble.

"No, I want you to go with me now." Her eyes remained fixed on me.

I opened her bedroom door. "I have bathwater running, let's talk about this when I get out of the tub."

While taking a bath I thought about our conversation. For eight months she'd done everything she could to destroy me while I tried to care for her, and now she wanted me to die with her. I hurt with my mom. I hurt for my mom. I hurt for our present situation and for what I knew would never be. So many years, so much hurt. But I had no intention of dying with her.

By the time I returned she was already asleep. She was unresponsive the last week of her life. Several major medical decisions had to be made, and I questioned the decisions I made even though I followed the advice of the hospice doctor and nurse. I'd taken care of her the best way I knew how. I can only guess it's natural to question the decisions made when faced with someone's life in your hands.

The emotional and physical exhaustion didn't let up. I stayed in the house and only went outside for short breaks. Puddy still came over during the day, and together we helped each other get through. At night alone with Mom, I slept on the couch so I could give her morphine every two hours and so I wouldn't wake Charlie. Even though she was unresponsive, I noticed she'd show signs of discomfort around the two to two-and-a-half-hour mark. If she looked comfortable, then I sat and waited in her room until it was time for another dose.

During her final days after I cleaned up the kitchen from supper, I would go to Mom's room and sit beside her bed or across the foot of the bed and watch TV or listen to the radio. I always told her when I walked in the room, "Mom, I'm here." Sometimes I'd talk to her, and other times I'd sit quietly with the volume barely audible. I often held her wrist to count her pulse and watch her chest. Her pulse was so slow, and her chest barely rose.

On Mom's last night, I sat beside her bed and listened to the radio. I looked down at the floor where I had a chicken egg on a heating pad. I had taken the egg away from the momma because the two previous chicks had not survived. As I sat there, I noticed the baby chick pecking its way out of the shell. I sat on the floor to watch. My back was to Mom's bedroom door. After a couple minutes, for absolutely no reason, I turned around to look at the door then turned back to my mom and said, "Mom, Charlie's here." Then I looked back down at the egg.

Immediately I thought, *Why did I say that?* I hadn't seen anyone standing in the doorway, and my stepdad, Charlie, had passed away six years previous. Five minutes later my mom began the final fight of her life. I hurried back to her side. I looked at the clock, but it wasn't time for her medication. I tried to call my sister, but she didn't answer. I screamed for my husband, but he had taken a sleep aid before he went to bed and never heard me. For nearly half an hour I rubbed my mom's head and told her it was okay. I told her I loved her. I told her she was not alone. Petrified, I felt like I couldn't breathe. I would have given anything not to be alone watching and hearing Mom fight a losing battle. After twenty minutes, Mom opened her eyes and took her last breath. With that breath, part of my world stopped.

For months after Mom passed, I mourned over her death and over the mother-daughter relationship that would never happen. Stepping off an eight-month roller-coaster ride of the fear, helplessness, panic, heartbreak, and sadness, I didn't know how to grasp my bearings. I didn't know what direction I needed to turn. During those months, I'd changed. My life had been on hold to take care of her, but I didn't know how to get back to the way my life had been before my mom became sick. I eventually realized I couldn't go back—the time had come to close the book on that part of my life and open the book to a new story.

My life beyond the scars.

Epilogue

The Joyful Heart Foundation estimates in the United States one in three women and one in four men are survivors of sexual violence. Every seventy-three seconds an American is sexually assaulted and three out of four cases go unreported to the police.[1] I'm one of those who didn't report mine. The Centers for Disease Control and Prevention (CDC) states 35 percent of women who were raped as minors were also raped as adults. More than half of female rape victims were raped by an intimate partner and 40 percent by an acquaintance.[2]

In the United States, a woman is assaulted or beaten every nine seconds. Worldwide, one in three women have been beaten or otherwise abused. Domestic violence is the leading cause of injury to women according to domesticviolencestatistics.org.[3]

These numbers are outrageously high, and victims often feel isolated and alone. Many believe no one understands the pain

---

1. "Sexual Assault and Rape Statistics," Joyful Heart Foundation, https://www .joyfulheartfoundation.org/learn/sexual-assault-and-rape/about-issue /who-does-sexual-assault-affect.

2. "Statistics," National Sexual Violence Resource Center, https://www .nsvrc.org/statistics.

3. "Domestic Violence Statistics," https://domesticviolencestatistics.org /domestic-violence-statistics/.

and shame, especially when it's the word of the victim against the abuser. Because of fear, victims often refuse or are unable to speak—fear no one will believe them or fear a family member will be harmed if the victim speaks up. Sometimes the fear may be the threat of more abuse.

In one long-term study, 80 percent of young adults who'd been abused were found to meet the diagnostic criteria for at least one psychiatric disorder, including depression, anxiety, post-traumatic stress disorder, dissociation, eating disorders, self-injury, suicide attempts, conduct disorder, and learning attention or memory difficulties.[4] According to HealthyPlace.com, 50 percent of individuals who engage in self-harm have been sexually abused, which is approximately two million cases reported annually in the United States.[5] The odds of attempting suicide are higher with a history of child abuse.

The abuse I faced sentenced me to twenty-six years of severe depression, post-traumatic stress disorder, self-harm, anxiety, numerous suicide attempts, and dissociation disorder.

There are as many women who have been abused as there are ones who have not. No one can truly understand the lasting effects of traumatic abuse unless experienced personally. Ignoring issues that make others uncomfortable or ones they don't understand doesn't help find a solution to the rising epidemic of abuse. Not discussing the issue is not an option.

---

4. "Long-Term Consequences of Child Abuse and Neglect," American Academy of Experts in Traumatic Stress, https://www.aaets.org/traumatic-stress-library/long-term-consequences-of-child-abuse-and-neglect.

5. Samantha Gluck, "Self Injury, Self Harm Statistics and Facts," Healthy Place, March 25, 2022, https://www.healthyplace.com/abuse/self-injury/self-injury-self-harm-statistics-and-facts.

Expecting a victim to move on because the abuse was in the past is asking them to turn off the pain, guilt, anger, hurt, and shame that's kept them prisoner. Victims don't need to be victimized again. I would like for others to understand that while, yes, pain can fade, it doesn't disappear. We are who we are because of our experiences. Our healing can take a lifetime of work.

Do I still struggle with the memories? Yes. The only difference now is how I respond to them. I no longer live in fear of my memories or fear of my actions toward myself. It's been a long and hard journey, but for the first time in my life I'm at peace. I will no longer allow my scars to haunt me, but that does not mean they're no longer there.

I share my scars, and my life, with others who have experienced abuse to show there is light at the end of the tunnel—there is hope, and they're not alone. Inner peace can be found, and there's no need to continue to torture and punish yourself. The past can't be fixed. No one can ever change the events that occurred or the pain suffered, but the future can be changed. In my pain I asked where God was. He showed me He had not moved or changed. He was always there; I was the one who moved away from Him.

As I've shared my story, others have shared their stories with me. Our stories may not be the same, but we carry scars, along with similarities in the psychological effects.

It's important we stand together and speak out. Our silence protects our abusers, destroying our lives and the lives of the people who love us. We need to work together to educate our communities about the effects of abuse. And I mean all forms of abuse, not just sexual, but emotional and physical abuse as well, which are just as damaging. It is time to change the stigma that we have been forced to carry, so that future generations won't have to suffer the way we did.

I have allowed my abusers victory over me for too many years, but now the victory will be mine! I will no longer be silent, and with God's help, I will see myself the way He does. I am not broken or alone. I am a daughter of the King.

If you enjoyed this book, will you consider sharing the message with others?

Let us know your thoughts. You can let the author know by visiting or sharing a photo of the cover on our social media pages or leaving a review at a retailer's site. All of it helps us get the message out!

Email: info@ironstreammmedia.com

 @ironstreammedia

Iron Stream, Iron Stream Fiction, Iron Stream Kids, Brookstone Publishing Group, and Life Bible Study are imprints of Iron Stream Media, which derives its name from Proverbs 27:17, "As iron sharpens iron, so one person sharpens another." This sharpening describes the process of discipleship, one to another. With this in mind, Iron Stream Media provides a variety of solutions for churches, ministry leaders, and nonprofits ranging from in-depth Bible study curriculum and Christian book publishing to custom publishing and consultative services.

For more information on ISM and its imprints, please visit IronStreamMedia.com